Food Safety

Food Safety

Victoria Sherrow

SERIES CONSULTING EDITOR
Alan Marzilli, M.A., J.D.

CHELSEA HOUSE
PUBLISHERS
An imprint of Infobase Publishing

Food Safety

Copyright © 2008 by Infobase Publishing

All rights reserved. No part of this book may be reproduced or utilized in any form or by any means, electronic or mechanical, including photocopying, recording, or by any information storage or retrieval systems, without permission in writing from the publisher. For information, contact:

Chelsea House
An imprint of Infobase Publishing
132 West 31st Street
New York, NY 10001

Library of Congress Cataloging-in-Publication Data

Sherrow, Victoria.
  Food safety / Victoria Sherrow.
      p. cm. — (Point/counterpoint)
  Includes bibliographical references and index.
  ISBN-13: 978-0-7910-9289-7 (hardcover)
  ISBN-10: 0-7910-9289-5 (hardcover)
  1. Food—Safety measures. 2. Food industry and trade—Safety measures. I. Title.
II. Series.

  TX531.S623 2007
  363.19'262—dc22   2007026652

Chelsea House books are available at special discounts when purchased in bulk quantities for businesses, associations, institutions, or sales promotions. Please call our Special Sales Department in New York at (212) 967-8800 or (800) 322-8755.

You can find Chelsea House on the World Wide Web at
http://www.chelseahouse.com

Series design by Keith Trego
Cover design by Keith Trego and Jooyoung An

Printed in the United States of America

Bang NMSG 10 9 8 7 6 5 4 3 2 1

This book is printed on acid-free paper.

All links and Web addresses were checked and verified to be correct at the time of publication. Because of the dynamic nature of the Web, some addresses and links may have changed since publication and may no longer be valid.

CONTENTS

Foreword
Alan Marzilli, M.A., J.D.
Washington, D.C.

The debates presented in Point/Counterpoint are among the most interesting and controversial in contemporary American society, but studying them is more than an academic activity. They affect every citizen; they are the issues that today's leaders debate and tomorrow's will decide. The reader may one day play a central role in resolving them.

Why study both sides of the debate? It's possible that the reader will not yet have formed any opinion at all on the subject of this volume—but this is unlikely. It is more likely that the reader will already hold an opinion, probably a strong one, and very probably one formed without full exposure to the arguments of the other side. It is rare to hear an argument presented in a balanced way, and it is easy to form an opinion on too little information; these books will help to fill in the informational gaps that can never be avoided. More important, though, is the practical function of the series: Skillful argumentation requires a thorough knowledge of *both* sides—though there are seldom only two, and only by knowing what an opponent is likely to assert can one form an articulate response.

Perhaps more important is that listening to the other side sometimes helps one to see an opponent's arguments in a more human way. For example, Sister Helen Prejean, one of the nation's most visible opponents of capital punishment, has been deeply affected by her interactions with the families of murder victims. Seeing the families' grief and pain, she understands much better why people support the death penalty, and she is able to carry out her advocacy with a greater sensitivity to the needs and beliefs of those who do not agree with her. Her relativism, in turn, lends credibility to her work. Dismissing the other side of the argument as totally without merit can be too easy—it is far more useful to understand the nature of the controversy and the reasons *why* the issue defies resolution.

The most controversial issues of all are often those that center on a constitutional right. The Bill of Rights—the first ten amendments to the U.S. Constitution—spells out some of the most fundamental rights that distinguish the governmental system of the United States from those that allow fewer (or other) freedoms. But the sparsely worded document is open to interpretation, and clauses of only a few words are often at the heart of national debates. The Bill of Rights was meant to protect individual liberties; but the needs of some individuals clash with those of society as a whole, and when this happens someone has to decide where to draw the line. Thus the Constitution becomes a battleground between the rights of individuals to do as they please and the responsibility of the government to protect its citizens. The First Amendment's guarantee of "freedom of speech," for example, leads to a number of difficult questions. Some forms of expression, such as burning an American flag, lead to public outrage—but nevertheless are said to be protected by the First Amendment. Other types of expression that most people find objectionable, such as sexually explicit material involving children, are not protected because they are considered harmful. The question is not only where to draw the line, but how to do this without infringing on the personal liberties on which the United States was built.

The Bill of Rights raises many other questions about individual rights and the societal "good." Is a prayer before a high school football game an "establishment of religion" prohibited by the First Amendment? Does the Second Amendment's promise of "the right to bear arms" include concealed handguns? Is stopping and frisking someone standing on a corner known to be frequented by drug dealers a form of "unreasonable search and seizure" in violation of the Fourth Amendment? Although the nine-member U.S. Supreme Court has the ultimate authority in interpreting the Constitution, its answers do not always satisfy the public. When a group of nine people—sometimes by a five-to-four vote—makes a decision that affects the lives of hundreds of millions, public outcry can be expected. And the composition of the Court does change over time, so even a landmark decision is not guaranteed to stand forever. The limits of constitutional protection are always in flux.

These issues make headlines, divide courts, and decide elections. They are the questions most worthy of national debate, and this series aims to cover them as thoroughly as possible. Each volume sets out some of the key arguments surrounding a particular issue, even some views that most people consider extreme or radical—but presents a balanced perspective on the issue. Excerpts from the relevant laws and judicial opinions and references to central concepts, source material, and advocacy groups help the reader to explore the issues even further and to read "the letter of the law" just as the legislatures and the courts have established it.

It may seem that some debates—such as those over capital punishment and abortion, debates with a strong moral component— will never be resolved. But American history offers numerous examples of controversies that once seemed insurmountable but now are effectively settled, even if only on the surface. Abolitionists met with widespread resistance to their efforts to end slavery, and the controversy over that issue threatened to cleave the nation in two; but today public debate over the merits of slavery would be unthinkable, though racial inequalities still plague the nation. Similarly unthinkable at one time was suffrage for women and minorities, but this is now a matter of course. Distributing information about contraception once was a crime. Societies change, and attitudes change, and new questions of social justice are raised constantly while the old ones fade into irrelevancy.

Whatever the root of the controversy, the books in POINT/ COUNTERPOINT seek to explain to the reader the origins of the debate, the current state of the law, and the arguments on both sides. The goal of the series is to inform the reader about the issues facing not only American politicians, but all of the nation's citizens, and to encourage the reader to become more actively involved in resolving these debates, as a voter, a concerned citizen, a journalist, an activist, or an elected official. Democracy is based on education, and every voice counts—so every opinion must be an informed one.

All of the volumes in the *Point-Counterpoint* series present both sides of a controversial issue, but this volume might change the way you eat. Widespread outbreaks of illnesses caused by the food we eat have grabbed headlines, but it is very difficult to know how to handle the news. Everything from snack food made with a spice imported from China to spinach grown organically in California has been implicated. Critics of the food industry and the government agencies that regulate it, such as the Food and Drug Administration (FDA) and the U.S. Department of Agriculture (USDA), argue that the government is subservient to powerful industry interests, and that the result is an unsafe food supply. Some of the main targets of criticisms discussed in this book are pesticides and other chemicals used in food production, genetically modified foods, and the practices of the meat and poultry industry. Many people, however, believe that the food supply in the United States is much safer, and food prices are kept lower, as a result of these practices. Additionally, the way that food is stored, prepared, and cooked has a major impact on safety. The U.S. government has a web site, www.foodsafety.gov, which offers individual consumers advice on how to reduce the risk of harm from foods.

Some of the material in this volume might seem alarming, as even supporters of the food industry do not maintain that the food supply is 100 percent safe. However, the debates focus on industry practices and regulations of what is sold, and consumers have a great deal of choice in what to buy and eat. For example, people can choose to buy organic food grown without chemical fertilizers, pesticides, or preservatives. However, because not everyone follows these precautions, the debate over farmers', manufacturers', and sellers' responsibility for food safety continues.

A Safe Food Supply?

For good health, people have long been told that eating more fruits and vegetables is vitally important. Not surprisingly, then, many consumers were concerned in August and September of 2006 when they heard that people had become ill from eating raw spinach. This spinach was contaminated with a strain of bacteria called *E. coli* 0157:H7. Severe cases of *E. coli* can cause a person's kidneys, pancreas, and other vital organs to fail. People may also suffer strokes, vision loss, or other disabling conditions.

Investigators from the U.S. Food and Drug Administration (FDA) found the same strain of *E. coli* at a cattle ranch in San Benito County, California, within a mile of the fields where the spinach was being raised.[1] Companies that sold spinach from these fields voluntarily recalled their products. The Centers for Disease Control and Prevention (CDC) later reported that the contaminated spinach caused 3 deaths and at least 4,000 cases of illness involving people in 26 states.[2]

This was no isolated event. Between 1995 and 2006, 20 outbreaks of *E. coli* were attributed to spinach or lettuce. Fruits can harbor dangerous bacteria, too. *E. coli* can contaminate apples on the ground that come into contact with infected animal feces.[3] In the fall of 1991, 23 people in Massachusetts became ill after drinking fresh, nonpasteurized apple cider.

Bacteria also turn up in meat. Four children died and at least 700 people became ill in late 1992 and early 1993 after eating hamburgers from a chain of restaurants in California, Idaho, Nevada, and Washington state.[4] The victims' symptoms included headaches, nausea, muscle weakness, fatigue, abdominal cramps, and diarrhea. The culprit was, again, *E. coli* 0157: H7. The ground beef used for the hamburgers was contaminated with infected cow feces, and the meat was not cooked long enough to kill the bacteria.

Other cases of food poisoning come from salmonella, a bacterium that can infect chickens, eggs, dairy products, and beef. In 1985, in one of the largest outbreaks of food poisoning in U.S. history, at least 2 people in the Chicago area died and more than 150,000 people became sick after drinking milk tainted with salmonella. Between 1985 and 1992, salmonella caused 437 outbreaks of illness, with 53 deaths.[5]

The Center for Science in the Public Interest has estimated that about 20,000 Americans get sick each day from some food they have eaten.[6] An estimated 76 million Americans suffer from food poisoning every year.[7] Experts say these numbers greatly underestimate the problem, because many episodes are never reported and people may not even know that food caused their illness. Statistics from the CDC show the main culprits are salmonella, *Staphylococcus aureus* (the most common cause of staph infections), *E. coli*, *Shigella*, *Clostridium botulinum* (causing botulism), listeria (causing Listeriosis), and campylobacter.[8]

Spinach farmer Dale Huss (right) and Doug Mosebar, president of the California Farm Bureau Federation, inspect spinach plants. In 2006, the FDA warned consumers not to purchase spinach after several people who ate packaged spinach were infected with *E. coli*.

Along with food-borne infections, there are concerns about seafood, drinking water, synthetic chemicals used for food production, hormones and antibiotics given to livestock, and bioengineered foods. The health impacts of these items may be less apparent than bacterial infections, but they are nonetheless important to consider.

The bioengineering of food in particular sparks heated debates. In 1998, for example, Dr. Arpad Pusztai, formerly of Scotland's Rowett Research Institute, reported on his research with genetically modified (GM) potatoes. Pusztai had spent three years examining the effects of genes that produce lectins in experimental potato plants. Lectins are plant proteins that bind with carbohydrate molecules. Pusztai's experiments showed that rats that ate the GM potatoes had stunted growth and weaker immune systems than rats that ate ordinary potatoes. Pusztai said that more testing was needed to confirm these early results but noted that he himself would avoid GM foods, adding, "It's very unfair to use our fellow citizens as guinea pigs."[9] GM critics, including Greenpeace and other environmental organizations, said that Pusztai's work confirmed the need to ban GM foods, while GM supporters criticized Pusztai's tests and called for extensive peer reviews of the data. The Rowett Research Institute fired Pusztai following the release of the report, charging that his findings were not supported by strong evidence.

Debates over food safety have even turned violent. Protesters in European countries have pulled GM crops out of the ground or used grenades to destroy places where GM crops were being tested. In 1998, scientists working outside Zurich, Switzerland, kept their GM rice seedlings in a bulletproof greenhouse.

Serious Concerns

Food is a universal human need, and people hope and expect that their foods will not hurt them. From coast to coast, Americans enjoy access to an array of meats and other animal products, grains, and thousands of frozen and packaged goods. Fresh fruits and vegetables are available year-round.

Debates about food safety have increased in recent decades as more people are examining the ways food is raised, stored, processed, shipped, handled, and prepared. In 1998 the International Foods Safety Council polled U.S. consumers, and 89 percent called food safety a "very important" national issue. Most ranked it above crime prevention. In the United States, various federal, state, and local agencies oversee food safety, and only 34 percent of the people polled by IFSC said that these agencies were doing an "excellent" job.[10] Critics claim that food safety laws are inadequate and often poorly enforced by these agencies;

they contend that federal agencies are set up in an outmoded and illogical manner that prevents them from operating in the most effective and efficient way.

As more people discuss food-borne, disease-causing microorganisms and other safety issues, the most common foods—apples, corn, eggs, milk, chicken, meats, fish—come under scrutiny. Even the containers that hold food products are suspect. For example, critics say that dioxin residues in some cardboard and plastic might endanger milk and other foods. Cans with seams that are sealed using lead have also been cause for worry.

Food Safety: A Brief History

People have long been concerned about the safety and purity of foods. Ancient Chinese texts warn people not to eat uncooked foods or foods that look or smell spoiled. By the Middle Ages, Europeans were making laws that banned bakers from selling bread that was made "impure" with fillers, such as ground peas or beans. Other laws set standards for foods, including weights and measurements, and authorized inspections. In North America in 1641, the Massachusetts Bay Colony passed a meat and fish inspection law.

People in years past realized that foods could cause illness, but they did not know why until nineteenth-century scientists learned about microorganisms. Powerful new microscopes enabled them to view bacteria and viruses that were invisible to the naked eye. With this knowledge, public health officials passed measures to improve sanitation and prevent the spread of infectious diseases. For example, based on the work of French bacteriologist Louis Pasteur, milk began to be put through a special heating process. After pasteurization became routine in the early 1900s, the number of deaths and illnesses due to contaminated milk declined sharply.

Meanwhile, the burgeoning chemical industry produced substances that could be added to foods to improve their appearance and shelf life. For centuries, people had used various naturally occurring substances to dye and/or preserve foods, even though some were poisonous. Concerns about chemical additives led to new laws. A statute enacted in England in 1875 declared: "No person shall mix, color, . . . or order or permit any other person to mix, color, . . . any article of food with any ingredient or material so as to render the article injurious to health."[11]

By the late 1800s, most food in the United States was no longer grown, produced, and distributed locally. Goods were often shipped to distant places and processed in manufacturing plants. The federal government took no active role in food safety, but some concerned scientists were testing foods on their own. One of these scientists was Dr. Peter Collier, chief chemist at the U.S. Department of Agriculture (USDA), which had been formed in 1862 to promote food production in the nation. Citing many problems in the foods he tested, Collier proposed a national food and drug safety law in 1880. But Congress defeated the law, and went on to defeat many similar bills between 1880 and 1915.

Collier's successor at the Department of Agriculture, Dr. Harvey W. Wiley, continued the effort. Wiley took charge in 1883 and was known as the father of the Food and Drug Act. He conducted studies that showed food adulteration was widespread, and under his leadership the federal government began testing more foods for pathogens and dangerous additives.

The meat industry came under fire as visitors to slaughterhouses described sick animals, overcrowding, foul odors, rats, and bloodstained floors. The Meat Inspection Act, passed in 1890, authorized the inspections of pigs and pork products raised for export. Pressure on the meat industry increased after author Upton Sinclair graphically depicted the Chicago stockyards in his 1906 novel *The Jungle*. In response, some meat packers began voluntary inspections of plants.

In 1906, Congress passed a more comprehensive federal Meat Inspection Act. USDA inspectors were assigned to each of the nation's 163 slaughterhouses and packing plants to check every animal before and after slaughter and packing. Sick or filthy animals were to be rejected and destroyed. Only meat that seemed healthy and unspoiled would be stamped as "inspected and passed." These inspections were visual and manual, with no laboratory testing, but rates of animal-borne infections in humans did decline after 1906. The law, however, did not give USDA inspectors the right to examine animals on the farm or

FROM THE BENCH

U.S. v. Lexington Mill & Elevator Co., 232 U.S. 399 (1914)

In 1914, the Supreme Court issued a ruling in *U.S. v. Lexington Mill & Elevator Co.,* a case involving food additives. The court stated that in order for bleached flour with nitrite residues to be banned from foods, the government must show a relationship between the chemical additive and the harm it poses to human health. The court also noted that the mere presence of such an ingredient was insufficient to make the food illegal.

Attorneys for the plaintiff (the U.S. government) argued:

> The fact that poisonous substances are to be found in the bodies of human beings, in the air, in potable water, and in articles of food, such as ham, bacon, fruits, certain vegetables, and other articles, does not justify the adding of the same or other poisonous substances to articles of food, such as flour, because the statute condemns the adding of poisonous substances. Therefore the court charges you that the government need not prove that this flour, or foodstuffs made by the use of it, would injure [232 U.S. 399, 408] the health of any consumer. It is the character—not the quantity—of the added substance, if any, which is to determine this case.

The court disagreed, saying, "The act has placed upon the government the burden of establishing, in order to secure a verdict of condemnation under this statute, that the added poisonous or deleterious substances must be such as may render such article injurious to health."

during transport, or to recall meat after it left the plant. The law also put the burden for proving meat was safe on the government, not the industry.

The Pure Food and Drug Act of 1906 went a step further and placed the responsibility for safety on food producers. It banned also interstate trade of mislabeled and/or adulterated foods, drugs, and drinks, but if the USDA found adulterations or misleading labels, it could not force manufacturers to stop selling the food. It could only seize the product, request a recall, and sue companies that refused to comply.

New laws addressed other concerns. In 1907, the Certified Colors List named seven coloring agents the government considered safe for food use. The Gould amendment of 1913 required that food be "plainly and conspicuously marked on the

THE LETTER OF THE LAW

The Federal Food, Drug, and Cosmetic Act

SEC. 301. [21 U.S.C. 331] The following acts and the causing thereof are hereby prohibited:

   (a) The introduction or delivery for introduction into interstate commerce of any food, drug, device, or cosmetic that is adulterated or misbranded.

   (b) The adulteration or misbranding of any food, drug, device, or cosmetic in interstate commerce.

   (c) The receipt in interstate commerce of any food, drug, device, or cosmetic that is adulterated or misbranded, and the delivery or proffered delivery thereof for pay or otherwise.

The Delaney clause of the Federal Food, Drug, and Cosmetic Act (1958) further provided, "No additive shall be deemed to be safe if it is found to induce cancer when ingested by man or laboratory animals or if it is found, after tests which are appropriate for the evaluation of the safety of food additives, to induce cancer in man or animals."

outside of the package in terms of weight, measure, or numerical count." In 1934, the U.S. Public Health Service proposed safety laws for restaurants and other commercial food services. The following year, it issued *An Ordinance Regulating Food and Drink Establishments*. Concerns about spoilage and declining sales led members of the seafood industry to seek voluntary inspections under the Seafood Inspection Act of 1934. Inspectors could examine a packer's premises, equipment, and processing methods. Products that passed inspection could advertise that fact on their labels.

In 1938, Congress passed the first Federal Food, Drug, and Cosmetics Act (FDCA), which expanded the scope of federal regulation and aimed to prevent the distribution of unsafe or deceptive products. It authorized the Food and Drug Administration (FDA) to inspect food manufacturing and processing facilities; monitor animal drugs, feeds, and veterinary devices; and set mandatory standards for foods, including bottled drinking water and infant formula. The law banned the sale of foods made under unsanitary conditions and required that the ingredients of nonstandard foods (food products with ingredients that vary from standards set by the government) be listed on labels. The definition of "adulteration" was expanded to include bacteria or chemicals that might harm consumers.[12] The act has been amended numerous times but remains the basis of federal food safety legislation.

"Big Agriculture" and Synthetic Chemicals

The twentieth century saw major changes in American lifestyles and demographics, along with new kinds of marketing techniques and methods of food production. Since ancient times, farmers have had to cope not only with the weather but also with insects, weeds, rodents, and other problems. Pests could destroy entire crops, and fertilizing and weeding large areas were laborious processes. Using chemicals developed for use during the two World Wars, companies made pesticides designed to kill or disable insects and other pests. The first pesticides were insecticides, followed by specific chemicals for specific classes of organisms: fungicides (mold and mildew), herbicides (weeds), miticides (mites), and rodenticides (rodents). Other chemicals were designed to fertilize soil with less labor. These chemicals were hailed as a boon to agriculture that could guarantee a large, steady food supply.

Two major categories of pesticides included organochlorines and organophosphates. DDT is one of the best-known organochlorines. During World War II, soldiers used powdered DDT to kill lice on their bodies. For agriculture, it was mixed with oil to make sprays. People later learned that this widely used substance has serious problems attached to it. For one, concentrated amounts of DDT can be deadly when the powder is mixed with oil. Also, DDT tends to accumulate in the fatty tissues, liver, and brain of people and animals.[13]

Along with other technology, the mass use of synthetic chemicals caused radical changes in agriculture. This new "industrial model" focused on higher yields at reduced costs, using chemicals for fertilizing and pest control. The use of pesticides for growing corn, for example, increased tenfold between 1950 and 1970, and the use of herbicides increased twentyfold.[14] The industrial approach also relied more on machines for harvesting, irrigating, and other tasks.

Many growers began specializing in one crop, such as soybeans or corn. By producing a single crop over large areas, they could reduce labor and maximize the use of specialized machines. At the same time, however, the widespread farming of only one crop has led to an imbalance in supply and demand. This means that though farmers are producing higher yields of corn and soybeans, they are not making more money doing it—and often they make less and sometimes wind up in bankruptcy.

Companies developed hybrid versions of corn and other crops by crossbreeding plants to make hardier varieties, and farmers began buying seed instead of producing their own. Widespread use of these seeds meant that crops became more uniform. This resulted in less plant diversity and a reduced gene pool as farmers planted fewer varieties and used hybrid seed. Pests that feed on a certain crop could multiply faster because they had a larger food supply. Insects eventually became resistant to pesticides and the chemicals that killed pests also killed their natural enemies. This rise in the number of pests led to what critics call the "pesticide treadmill." Statistics show that the use of pesticides increased by 1,000 percent between 1947 and 1974.[15] In addition to problems with controlling pests, chemicals deplete soil quality faster, requiring additional fertilizer.

As agriculture became industrialized, people began referring to the seed industry, fertilizer and pesticide companies, and makers of farm machinery as "agribusiness." The family farm system gave way to large, corporate-run farms, putting the control over food production into the hands of fewer people.

Debates Over Chemicals and Health

During the 1950s, some scientists warned that agricultural chemicals endanger people's health and the environment. In her landmark book *Silent Spring* (1962), biologist Rachel Carson discussed the impact of chemicals on the ecosystem and balance of nature. She showed how DDT, lindane, chlordane, and other chemicals had killed wildlife while polluting the air, soil, and waters in areas where they were sprayed on crops. Carson urged that pesticides and other chemicals be used with extreme caution and precision, and only after considering the wide-ranging impact. For their part, chemical companies said their products were safe for use and vital to feed an ever-growing population. Food producers said these chemicals enabled them to produce foods at reasonable prices for consumers.

Carson's book roused intense opposition to DDT. In 1967, the Environmental Defense Fund (EDF) began filing lawsuits, state by state. This was followed by a federal lawsuit against pesticide use. In 1972, Congress passed the Federal Pest Control Act, which banned DDT, among other substances.

Some 400 chemicals were in use in 1972 when the federal Environmental Protection Agency (EPA) was authorized to regulate them under the Insecticide, Fungicide and Rodenticide Act (FIFRA). Founded in 1969, the EPA, along with state agencies, was tasked with enforcing pesticide laws. Staffing was limited, however, and about 12 inspectors might be assigned to thousands of farms. Years passed before some products were examined or Congress set stricter standards for evaluating chemicals that were approved decades earlier. By 1989, the FDA had gathered data on 192 of the older chemicals but had fully reviewed and reregistered only 2 of them.[16] Such studies can take years as scientists examine the effects of a pesticide on test animals.

During the 1980s, the media focused more attention on food safety, and consumer and environmental groups became more active. A poll taken in March 1989 showed that 73 percent of Americans preferred fewer pesticides and chemicals on food even if food prices increased.[17]

Concerns about pesticides led to more lawsuits. In *California v. Browner*, the state of California joined labor organizations and environmental groups to sue the federal government (namely, EPA administrator Carol M. Browner). They based their case on the Delaney clause of the Food, Drug, and Cosmetic Act, which prohibited any cancer-causing substance, in any amount, from being added to processed foods. But EPA policy permitted questionable pesticides if the substances posed what was considered a negligible risk. The plaintiffs in the case said the Delaney clause banned *all* such substances. This suit was settled in 1994 when the EPA agreed to take action against up to 36 pesticides within two years. These pesticides, which caused cancer in laboratory animals, were still present in canned vegetables and juices, among other products. The EPA stated that carcinogenic pesticides had already been removed from food use. At the same time, it asked Congress to revise laws in ways that addressed all health risks, not just cancer. Administrator

Browner commented, "The entire food safety program requires overhaul."[18]

Juanita D. Duggan, vice president of the National Food Producers Association, said that the pesticides named in the lawsuit were safe for use and that this case took the Delaney clause "to its irrational, illogical extreme."[19] Speaking for the other side, Al Meyerhoff, a lawyer for the National Resources Defense Council, called the decision "a critical breakthrough for public health."[20]

As of 2007, the FDA, EPA, and Food Safety and Inspection Service (FSIS) of the U.S. Department of Agriculture share responsibility for deciding whether pesticide residues pose health risks. The EPA reviews scientific data before registering a product for use and establishes a "tolerance" level for registered products. The FDA enforces those levels on some foods, while meat, poultry, and eggs come under the USDA's jurisdiction. Together the FDA and EPA set "action levels"—enforcement guidelines—in regard to pesticides that have been banned but whose residues remain in the environment (for example, DDT). These policies aim to protect the public, but later chapters in this book will show that the debate continues.

Recent Legislation

In recent decades, new food-related laws have been debated and passed, along with amendments to the 1938 Food, Drug, and Cosmetics Act. The Nutrition Labeling and Education Act of 1990 requires companies to list the contents and nutritional value of packaged foods, including the percentage of Recommended Daily Amounts (RDAs) of vitamins and minerals, calories, grams of fat, and other information. The food industry opposed this law, citing costs and other concerns, but supporters say that detailed labels help consumers avoid allergic reactions and eat healthier, safer diets.

The FDA has penalized companies for deceptive or misleading labels. After a manufacturer refused to reword its labels, the FDA seized thousands of cartons of orange juice labeled as

"Fresh Choice" even though the juice was made from concentrate.[21] Other inspections have found false claims of "no cholesterol" on labels. Consuming foods high in cholesterol could harm people with heart disease who eat low-cholesterol diets.

Concerns over meat safety rose in the 1990s after people died from eating hamburgers contaminated with *E. coli*. Nancy Donley's son Alex was one of the victims; in 1995, she spoke out to Congress, saying, "Meat inspection hasn't significantly changed since 1906!" Donley and others called for tougher sanitation standards and microbial testing. They said federal officials should have the means and authority to track down the source of adulterated or contaminated products and recall them immediately. "There is very little food safety research," Donley pointed out. "No one knows for sure how many people are afflicted and/or die from food-borne illness. The USDA estimates range from 6.5 to 30 million."[22]

In 1996, the USDA instituted a new program that aims to remedy shortcomings in traditional inspection methods. The Hazard Analysis and Critical Control Points (HACCP) system, which will be discussed later, emphasizes prevention and puts more responsibility on the industry itself. The government required that all 6,500 meat and poultry processing plants in the United States adopt a HACCP system. Seafood processing facilities were required to install HACCP plans by 1997, and producers of fruit and vegetable juices had to adopt HACCP by 2004.

Also in 1996, Congress endorsed the Food Quality Protection Act (FQPA), which changed the way the EPA regulates pesticides used in food production. The FQPA required that an additional safety factor be used when calculating tolerance levels for infants and children. This law requires the EPA to review pesticide registrations regularly to ensure that all products meet updated safety standards. It eliminated the Delaney clause and substituted a new safety standard: "a reasonable certainty that no harm" will result from all combined sources of exposure to pesticides, including drinking water.[23]

In 2000, President Bill Clinton's Food Safety Initiative aimed to coordinate activities of the FDA, CDC, USDA, state governments, academia, and industry. The initiative urged them to work together to develop and apply nationwide food safety standards, implement the HACCP system, and improve testing methodologies for bacteria, among other things.

Despite these changes, critics say the responsibilities of various food safety agencies still overlap in illogical ways. Author Marion Nestle points out some of the results that may occur:

> Under the current system, a sandwich made with bread, ham, cheese, lettuce, and tomato raises regulatory issues of terrifying complexity. If the sandwich is made with one slice of bread, it falls under USDA rules [because it is considered a meat or poultry item]; if it is made with two slices, it is the FDA's responsibility [because the meat is not visible]. . . . [T]hree cabinet-level federal agencies—the FDA, EPA, and USDA (including four major divisions of the latter)—oversee its farm-to-table production. . . . State inspectors add a third level of inconsistent oversight."[24]

Summary

Although few Americans follow the workings of government regulatory systems, news reports about tainted spinach, meats, peanut butter, and other foods have convinced many people that they cannot take food safety for granted. They wonder if there is enough information reported, and whom to believe. Other people believe their food is safe—or at least as safe as is possible—and that laws and food safety agencies are effective.

Debates over food safety take place in homes, educational and research institutions, farms, factories, businesses, and government settings. These complex debates are influenced by politics, economics, science, and technological developments, as well as attitudes, values, and beliefs. For instance, vegetarians may avoid meat because they object to the way livestock are treated. Some people buy organic produce because they believe pesticides harm the environment and farm workers. Some opponents of bioengineered food say people have no right to "play God" by trying to control nature.

As this book will show, even experts disagree about how to ensure a safe and adequate food supply. Organizations that support opposing sides lobby Congress and file lawsuits to promote their causes. As a result, changes often come slowly. Laws and policies usually reflect an attempt to balance various interests—including the companies that produce seeds and agricultural chemicals, growers, livestock farmers and ranchers, food processors, consumers, the environment, and the food needs of developing nations.

The following chapters will discuss several controversial issues involving food safety, showing the viewpoints on both sides. Each debate raises certain specific questions, as well as one overriding question: Who decides what is safe, and on what basis?

Using Pesticides and Other Chemicals in Food Production Poses Health Risks for Consumers

Early in 1989, the National Resources Defense Council (NRDC) issued a report that triggered a national debate about food safety. The report stated that 5,500 to 6,200 children of preschool age—about 1 in every 3,400 children between ages one and five—might eventually get cancer resulting from chemical residues on the fruits and vegetables in their diets. The report cited 23 pesticides, including daminozide, trade name Alar.[25] First used in 1968, Alar was sprayed on apples to keep them from dropping off the tree before they ripened, thus improving color, firmness, and shelf life. The report explained that daminozide breaks down into UDMH, a suspected carcinogen. And it penetrates the peel, so it cannot be completely washed off.

The CBS news program *60 Minutes* discussed this report, focusing on Alar use in apple farming. Other journalists joined in, noting that the EPA had concluded that exposure to Alar/ UDMH over a lifetime could result in 45 cases of cancer per 1 million people—45 times the risk the EPA considers "acceptable."[26] The apple industry argued that Alar was safe and, besides, it was used on less than 15 percent of the apple crop.

At that time, Alar was only one of about 50,000 pesticide products—including insecticides, herbicides, and fungicides— in use. Federal guidelines told growers which pesticides they could use and for what purposes. For example, about 50 different pesticides were permitted on broccoli. Apples were typically treated with 3 fungicides and daminozide.[27]

In the wake of the reports regarding Alar, many people discarded apples they had bought and thousands of schools removed apples and apple products from cafeteria menus. Sales of organic produce surged. Stores declared they would not sell

THE LETTER OF THE LAW

Federal Insecticide, Fungicide, and Rodenticide Act (FIFRA)

Subchapter II—Environmental Pesticide Control

Sec. 136a. Registration of pesticides

(a) Requirement of registration

Except as provided by this subchapter, no person in any State may distribute or sell to any person any pesticide that is not registered under this subchapter. To the extent necessary to prevent unreasonable adverse effects on the environment, the Administrator may by regulation limit the distribution, sale, or use in any State of any pesticide that is not registered under this subchapter and that is not the subject of an experimental use permit under section 136c of this title or an emergency exemption under section 136p of this title.

apples treated with Alar. Later that year, the company that made Alar voluntarily canceled its use in food. Although supporters of Alar claimed that a person would need to eat tons of apples in his or her lifetime to face any risk, opponents said no risk is acceptable, especially since it is possible to avoid such chemicals.

Other pesticides have come under fire, too. Heptachlor, a toxic organochlorine compound, was used on crops from 1948 until 1978, when the EPA banned it for all uses except termite control. Pineapple companies in Hawaii, however, received an extension to use heptachlor. Pineapple leaves wound up being fed to Hawaiian cattle, and in 1982, unsafe levels of heptachlor were detected in milk.[28] After a 1987 study, the EPA stated that heptachlor still posed a cancer risk because it contaminates the air, even when used as directed for termite control. Manufacturers agreed to stop selling it, but the EPA allowed pest control companies to use their remaining supplies, so heptachlor was used in thousands more homes and other locations. In 1989, a large poultry company in Arkansas had to destroy 400,000 chickens after they ingested animal feed that had been illegally treated with heptachlor. And nearly 100 dairy farms in three states were shut down after unsafe levels of heptachlor appeared in the cows' milk.[29]

Sometimes tainted products still reach consumers, as occurred in 1994 with more than a million boxes of cereal. Chlorpyrifos, a pesticide that is not approved for use in food products, was used to treat 21 million bushels of oats, which were in turn used to make various foods.[30]

These examples show problems that occur when synthetic chemicals are used in food production. Critics worry about illegal use and accidents, as well as legal products considered by some to be unsafe. There are complaints that regulatory agencies do not adequately test pesticides before registering them for use, and that regulations are not enforced quickly, nor strictly enough. Since agribusinesses focus first and foremost on food production and profits, companies may not take enough precautions to protect consumers from these chemicals.

Exposure to pesticides has been linked with cancer and other health problems.

Chemicals used to grow crops, store foods, and improve the appearance of foods have been linked to numerous health problems, including cancer, miscarriages, birth defects, nervous system damage, learning disabilities, and hyperactivity in children. Scientists believe pesticides can disrupt body functions by causing abnormal cell division and interfering with the replication and repair of DNA. Pesticides also seem to inhibit the hormones that help to regulate the nervous system. Exposure to pesticides can lower the body's immunity, as well, since toxic chemicals burden the liver, the organ that plays a major role in eliminating toxins from the body.

Scientists have documented the effects of specific pesticides, including three toxic organochlorines: DDT, chlordane, and heptachlor. Introduced in the 1940s, all three were applied to fruit, vegetable, and tobacco crops. Chlordane was used in lawn care, and both chlordane and heptachlor were used against termites. These products can enter the body by air and skin and then accumulate in fatty tissues and organs. They have been linked to liver disease and cancers, including brain tumors. All three were later banned—DDT in 1972; chlordane and heptachlor in 1987—but they are not biodegradable and so will remain in the environment for decades.

Another major class of pesticides known as organophosphates come from the same family of chemicals as nerve gas. Scientists believe these chemicals damage the brain and nervous system by causing neurons to over-fire, which can trigger seizures, convulsions, and other symptoms, as well as unpredictable long-term damage. Dieldrin, aldrin, endrin, and others in this group have caused liver cancer, nerve damage, birth defects, sterility, and other problems in animals.[31]

Many concerns about pesticides involve cancer. In a 1987 report, the National Academy of Sciences estimated that pesticides could account for 6,000 of the 4 million cancer cases diagnosed each year.[32] From time to time, the EPA has classified

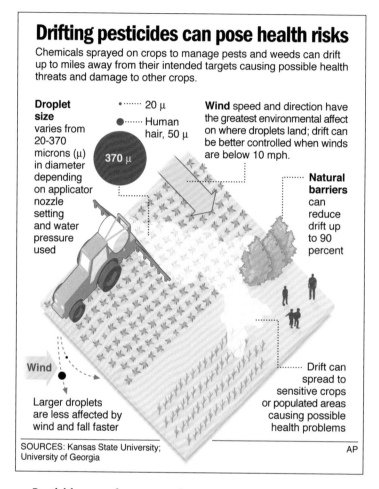

Drifting pesticides can pose health risks

Chemicals sprayed on crops to manage pests and weeds can drift up to miles away from their intended targets causing possible health threats and damage to other crops.

Droplet size varies from 20-370 microns (μ) in diameter depending on applicator nozzle setting and water pressure used

······· 20 μ
●······ Human hair, 50 μ
370 μ

Wind speed and direction have the greatest environmental affect on where droplets land; drift can be better controlled when winds are below 10 mph.

Natural barriers can reduce drift up to 90 percent

Wind

Larger droplets are less affected by wind and fall faster

Drift can spread to sensitive crops or populated areas causing possible health problems

SOURCES: Kansas State University; University of Georgia

AP

Pesticides are often sprayed on crops to prevent insects from eating them. The spraying process, however, allows a certain amount of the chemical to drift away from its intended target, often landing in spaces used for other activities, like playgrounds and athletic fields.

dozens of the active ingredients in pesticides as probable or possible human carcinogens.[33] The agency also said "pesticide residues pose the third highest threat of environmentally induced cancer, behind cigarettes and radon."[34]

Scientists find higher rates of various cancers, birth defects, and miscarriage among adults and children who work among crops sprayed with pesticides; this includes farmers and their families in particular.[35] The National Cancer Institute (NCI) studied links between the use of the herbicide 2,4-D and rates of non-Hodgkins lymphoma, a cancer in the blood. When people were exposed for more than 20 days per year, 2,4-D was associated with a three-fold increase in risk for Nebraska farmers and a six-fold increase for farmers in Kansas. Flour mill employees, who often use pesticides to disinfect flour, also faced greater than average risks. Canadian researchers found that rates for Parkinson's disease were six times higher in the major agricultural region of Quebec province than they were in areas with the least pesticide use.[36] In addition, more than 650 farm workers in the United States were diagnosed with parathion poisoning between 1960 and 1990; 100 died.[37] In 1999, parathion, an insecticide, was banned from agricultural use. Accidents also occur, sometimes through inadvertent exposure to chemicals that were sprayed. The American Association of Poison Control Centers estimated that in 2002, 69,000 children suffered from pesticide-related poisoning or exposure to poisonous pesticides.[38]

In looking for causes of breast cancer, in particular, scientists have considered genetic predisposition, diet, hormonal influences, and environmental toxins, including pesticides. PCBs (polychlorinated biphenyls) and DDT tend to accumulate in fatty tissue, including the fatty tissue of the breast. These substances or their broken-down products can mimic the activity of estrogen in the body, and have been linked to the development of breast tumors in animals. Excessive amounts of estrogen might spur the growth of breast and uterine tumors and aggravate endometriosis (growths of uterine tissue outside the uterus). A study published in the *Archives of Environmental Health* showed 50 to 60 percent higher levels of DDT in women who had breast cancer compared to women who did not.[39] Other studies have shown higher concentrations of the organochlorines DDT, DDE, or PCBs in the fat tissue of breast cancer victims. Breast cancer is the most common cancer among women and the leading cause of death in women aged 35 to 54.

Pesticides can also endanger a developing fetus. Exposure to dioxins may lead to reproductive abnormalities and genetic mutations, as well as damage to the immune system. Dioxin, a chemical by-product of certain herbicides, was widely used during the 1960s and 1970s. Dead and deformed wild animals, including fish and birds, were found in and near sprayed areas. Dioxin was finally banned in 1985 but it still turns up in water, animal feed, and foods.[40]

Regulatory agencies and lawmakers must do more to protect consumers.

In setting "tolerance levels" for pesticide residues, the EPA considers the maximum amount that would be present on foods when growers follow the manufacturer's directions. The EPA then calculates a tolerance level for that pesticide measured in parts per million. These limits reflect health data from pesticide manufacturers and researchers who conduct animal studies. Critics say these tests are often inadequate and rely too much on testing done by pesticide producers, who by definition may not be impartial. Critics also believe these legal limits are set too high and underestimate people's exposure, since Americans today eat more fruits and vegetables per day than previous generations ate. People today are exposed to chemical residues in water and air, as well as in food, so the exposure is both chronic and cumulative.

In its 1989 publication *Pesticides in Children's Food*, the National Resources Defense Council (NRDC) noted dangerous gaps in the regulatory system, including inadequate sampling and testing procedures, and failure to consider children's eating patterns or susceptibility when setting legal limits on pesticide residues. Children usually eat more fruits and vegetables relative to their body weight, and their developing bodies are more vulnerable than adult bodies.[41] This problem was not addressed until the Food Quality Protection Act of 1996 (FQPA) took effect. It required the EPA to reassess the amount of residues it permits on food and the tolerance levels, specifically considering the unique vulnerability of children. The FQPA also required the EPA to review and reregister pesticides used in food production. By 2006, the EPA had completed 99 percent of this task and expected to fully complete it by October 2008.

The FDA is authorized to monitor and enforce laws regarding pesticides and inspect random samples of produce for residues. Critics say, however, inspections are inadequate, both in number and frequency. Each year the FDA samples less than

FROM THE BENCH

Les v. Reilly, U.S. Court of Appeals, Ninth Circuit. 968 F.2d 985 (1992)

A group of citizens including Kathleen E. Les joined environmental groups and the AFL-CIO to sue the EPA for permitting the use of four pesticides that had been shown to cause cancer. They based their case on the Delaney clause, which took effect in 1958. The court ruled in the plaintiffs' favor, saying:

The language is clear and mandatory. The Delaney clause provides that no additive shall be deemed safe if it induces cancer. 21 U.S.C. 348(c)(3). The EPA states in its final order that appropriate tests have established that the pesticides at issue here induce cancer in humans or animals. 56 Fed.Reg. at 7774–75. The statute provides that once the finding of carcinogenicity is made, the EPA has no discretion. As a leading work on food and drug regulation notes:

"[T]he Delaney Clause leaves the FDA room for scientific judgment in deciding whether its conditions are met by a food additive. But the clause affords no flexibility once FDA scientists determine that these conditions are satisfied. A food additive that has been found in an appropriate test to induce cancer in laboratory animals may not be approved for use in food for any purpose, at any level, regardless of any 'benefits' that it might provide."

one percent of the nation's food supply.[42] On-site produce inspections went from 4,573 in 2005 to about 3,400 in 2006.[43] The government cannot assume that growers will comply with the manufacturers' instructions or EPA regulations. Violations and accidents can and do occur, which means that contaminated foods can reach consumers. And, according to the Center for Science in the Public Interest, the FDA "lacks authority to detain domestic food suspected of containing illegal residues while it is seeking either a seizure or injunction in order to remove the food from the market."[44]

The FDA states its policy this way:

> The agency may request a product recall if the firm is not willing to remove dangerous products from the market without FDA's written request. Only when a medical device, human tissue products, and infant formula pose a risk to human health; that the law specifically authorizes FDA to prescribe a recall and to rule on the scope and extent of the same.[45]

Adding even more complications, fruits and vegetables are imported from countries where laws governing pesticides are more lenient than U.S. laws. Produce often comes from Latin America, primarily Mexico, Chile, Ecuador, and Brazil. Meats, seafood, poultry, coffee, cheese, and other products also are imported. Critics say the FDA needs more information about the chemicals used by foreign food suppliers.

When the agency and legislators do act, the changes in laws and regulations come too slowly. Critics were condemning DDT in the early 1950s, but it was not banned until 1972. Although some European countries had banned the use of chlordane in 1958, the United States did not even restrict its use until 1975. After the Federal Insecticide, Fungicide and Rodenticide Act (FIFRA) of 1972, the EPA proceeded to re-examine 600 farm chemicals already in use. By 1987, it had canceled only 5, gathered data on 30, and was accumulating information on about 120 others.[46] In the case of the pesticide carbofuran, environmentalists and scientists complained for more than 20 years before the EPA banned the use of the chemical for most purposes in 2006. In the meantime, it killed millions of birds and tainted foods and drinking water.[47] Both the EPA and FDA have said they need more funding and employees to perform their duties.

According to many critics, lobbying by the powerful food industry often prevents stronger safety laws. Author Sheila Kaplan describes a "triumvirate made up of the chemical companies that manufacture $6.5 billion worth of farm chemicals a year, the agribusiness giants who use them, and the grocery manufacturers who process the food and turn it into products . . . They include some of the biggest and best known businesses in the country."[48]

People expressed mixed reactions in 2002 when the George W. Bush administration announced new policies regarding food safety. They allowed the EPA to review pesticides and remove those they considered risky somewhat faster than in the past; but they eliminated the Delaney clause, which banned the use of any carcinogenic chemical in processed foods. The new standard for determining risk became a tolerance level of 1 in 1 million, meaning that a pesticide can be used if it causes a risk below 1 case per 1 million people over a lifetime. Critics also opposed the provision that bans states from applying stricter standards than the federal government does toward pesticide residues.

Some progress occurred in 2006. After completing the reviews Congress had mandated in 1996, the EPA canceled nearly 4,400 product registrations, leaving 17,592 allowable products. Still, many people remain concerned and want federal agencies to rethink their policies regarding "acceptable risk." Critics also call for closer examination of pesticide synergy, or how mixtures of pesticides interact together and with other chemicals, as well as what happens when chemicals converge in bodies of water. Many are demanding more thorough and frequent inspections, too. They say the government should actively encourage food producers to reduce or eliminate pesticides and offer those producers at least as much economic support as they give conventional (nonorganic) farmers.

Pesticides may be ineffective and their use results in resistant strains of insects and weeds.

Do insecticides truly prevent pests from destroying crops? Statistics paint a different picture. Although growers applied 10 times more chemicals in the 1980s than growers used in the 1940s, insects were destroying more crops. By 1990, farmers were using more than 30 times more tons of pesticides than their counterparts in 1945, yet they lost 20 percent more of their harvests.[49]

Such damage can occur because insecticides kill natural predators of crop pests, and also because insects eventually grow

César Chávez

In 1986, social activist and union organizer César Chávez (1927–1993) launched his "Grapes of Wrath" campaign to publicize the problems of pesticide exposure and poor working conditions endured by adults and children who worked picking grapes.

Born in Arizona, Chávez grew up laboring in the fields of California after his family members became migrant workers in 1937. He later served in the Navy and began working in 1962 to raise public awareness about the problems of farm workers, spreading his message through peaceful protests, organizing the United Farm Workers of America (UFA), petitioning the government, and fasting. At times, Chávez asked people to boycott grapes, lettuce, and other crops until growers agreed to improve conditions for farm workers.

At age 61, in 1988, Chávez fasted for 36 days, the longest and last of his fasts. He led another protest march in February 1990 after 25-year-old Jose Campos Martinez died of methyl parathion poisoning while carrying out his job applying this insecticide to almond trees in Kern County, California.

resistant to the insecticide in order to survive. The National Academy of Sciences (NAS) has noted a large increase in the number of chemically resistant insects: Before 1945, when few chemical insecticides were used, just 7 species of insects and mites were known to be resistant. By 1984, that number was at least 447.[50] A similar process occurs with plant pests. Herbicides prevent cell functions in weeds, causing them to die. But, like insects, invasive plants can adapt and evolve into forms that withstand herbicides. Intensive farming practices based on pesticide use also lead to crop crowding, which results in still more weeds and pests. To deal with these problems, growers may use still more chemicals, and companies make new products to kill the resistant strains. These strains will also eventually resist the new chemicals, creating a vicious cycle.

On top of this, pesticide sprays often do not even reach their target. The Center for Science in the Public Interest (CSPI) estimated that less than one percent of the billions of pounds applied to fields annually reach the pests themselves; the rest goes into land, water, air, and food.[51] Dr. Gary Null, a public health scientist, sums up the problem: "This addiction to synthetic pesticides has created a nearly billion-dollar industry that manufactures products that over the long run are ineffective and endanger our entire environment."[52]

Pesticides cause costly environmental damage.

Pesticides not only endanger food but also cause environmental problems that further impact health. They harm fish, wildlife, and livestock, kill bees that pollinate plants, and destroy natural vegetation. Soil erosion can occur when conventional farming treats the soil as a place to hold plants up vertically for chemicals applications. The USDA estimated that about one billion metric tons of topsoil were lost from U.S. farmland in 2000.[53] Soil erosion means that more pesticide-laden soil can enter, and pollute, water.

Industrial agriculture is the leading cause of water pollution in the United States, and EPA surveys of groundwater consistently find pesticides. As biologist Rachel Carson wrote in 1962, "pollution of the groundwater is pollution of water everywhere."[54] In areas near heavy agricultural activity, people have reported that their tap water smelled foul and turned colors, and that their families suffered from numerous health problems.[55] An estimated 10 percent of community water and 4 percent of rural drinking water contains one or more pesticides, including DBCP and aldicarb.[56]

Experts have estimated the social and environmental costs of pesticide use at about $1 billion every year. These costs include human and animal pesticide poisonings, contaminated livestock products, the reduced number of natural enemies and pesticide resistance, honey bee poisonings and the resulting decrease in pollination, losses of crops and trees, fishery and wildlife losses, and the cost of government pesticide pollution controls.[57]

Growers can choose safer pest-control methods that benefit consumers and the environment.

Safe and effective pest-control solutions are available. Many growers use sustainable agriculture methods to protect natural resources, treat animals humanely, and ensure healthy workers. In 1990, the U.S. government defined sustainable agriculture as "an integrated system of plant and animal production practices" that aim to

> satisfy human food and fiber needs; enhance environmental quality and the natural resource base upon which the agricultural economy depends; make the most efficient use of nonrenewable resources and on-farm resources and integrate, where appropriate, natural biological cycles and controls; sustain the economic viability of farm operations; and enhance the quality of life for farmers and society as a whole.[58]

Would crop yields plummet if people limit or avoid synthetic chemicals? After examining projects in seven countries in

Europe and North America, Jules Pretty, director of the Centre for Environment and Society at the University of Essex, disputes this belief:

> Farmers are finding that they can cut their inputs of costly pesticides and fertilisers substantially, varying from 20–80%, and be financially better off. Yields do fall to begin with (by 10–15% typically), but there is compelling evidence that they soon rise and go on increasing. In the USA, for example, the top quarter sustainable agriculture farmers now have higher yields than conventional farmers, as well as a much lower negative impact on the environment.[59]

Farmers who keep using pesticides can reduce their use by starting with biological controls and using chemicals only to save a crop. Principles of Integrated Pest Management (IPM) help them to choose pest-resistant plants. Crop rotation can minimize pests and promote healthier soil. Weeding machines and mulch will control weeds without chemicals. Traps baited with special substances can attract pests—for example, sex attractants for boll weevils—and vacuum equipment can suck insects off plants.

These methods are profitable as well as safe. California grape rancher Don Goldberg reduced his pesticide use by 75 percent during the 1980s by using what he called "a holistic system."[60] Goldberg introduced beneficial insects, such as the green lacewing, which eats mealybugs, mites, and worms. He also built taller, wider plant trellises to promote air circulation and reduce fungal growth. Planting grasses and flowers between rows of grapes provided nitrogen for the soil, thus reducing the need for fertilizer.

Biological controls in the form of a pest's natural enemies have proven their effectiveness, too. When the cottony-cushion scale threatened California citrus trees in 1889, Vedalia beetles from Australia were used to kill them without harming the trees or fruit. In the 1920s, a type of wasp helped to control

Oriental fruit moths. In 1946, scientists introduced Chryso-lina beetles to California and the Pacific Northwest, where the Klamath weed was invading millions of acres of rangeland. The beetles killed the weed, restoring about 99 percent of the endangered land. Ladybugs destroy various pests, too, including the eggs of worms that eat lettuce and cabbage. The number of insectaries—businesses that breed beneficial insects for farmers—has been increasing as more people realize the benefits of this kind of pest control.

Effective pesticides also can be made without hazardous chemicals. Since the 1980s, the market for natural pesticides has grown as people seek products that do not harm animals and break down quickly. One product, made with parasites, kills crop-eating grasshoppers. Others made with bacteria kill plant-eating worms, moths, beetles, insects, or fungi. Some products work by producing microorganisms in the soil that

THE LETTER OF THE LAW

Public Law 104–170, title III, Sec. 303, Aug. 3, 1996, 110 Stat. 1512

The Secretary of Agriculture, in cooperation with the Administrator, shall implement research, demonstration, and education programs to support adoption of Integrated Pest Management. Integrated Pest Management is a sustainable approach to managing pests by combining biological, cultural, physical, and chemical tools in a way that minimizes economic, health, and environmental risks. The Secretary of Agriculture and the Administrator shall make information on Integrated Pest Management widely available to pesticide users, including Federal agencies. Federal agencies shall use Integrated Pest Management techniques in carrying out pest management activities and shall promote Integrated Pest Management through procurement and regulatory policies, and other activities.

destroy nematodes, tiny wormlike creatures that feed on plant roots.

The environmental benefits come with a financial benefit. Researchers have estimated the annual savings that can result by switching either completely or partially to biological controls in food production. The estimates include $4 million in the control of the black scale and citrophilous mealybug that attack citrus crops in California; $8 million saved in controlling the alfalfa weevil in middle Atlantic states; and $13 million for the alfalfa blotch leafminer in Northeastern United States.[61]

Federal Organic Standards

In 2000, the U.S. Department of Agriculture (USDA) issued standards for the use of the word "organic" in food labeling. These standards ban the use of most synthetic (and petroleum derived) pesticides and fertilizers, and all antibiotics, genetic engineering, irradiation, and sewage sludge in the production of fruits, vegetables, meat, and poultry. In order to be labeled organic, livestock must eat 100 percent organic feed that is free of animal byproducts or growth hormones. The animals also must have access to the outdoors, although they may have limited access to outdoors and still meet the standard. Labels for organic foods include these variations:

- 100 percent organic: Contains only organically produced ingredients

- Organic: 95 percent of the ingredients must be organically grown and the remaining 5 percent must come from nonorganic ingredients that have been approved by the National Organics Standards Board

- Made with organic ingredients: A product containing no less than 70 percent organic ingredients

Source: The Consumers Union Guide to Environmental Labels, www.eco-labels.org.

Although organic farming was once disparaged as old-fashioned, inefficient, and costly, viewpoints have changed. In a 1980 report that recommended expanding research and education to boost organic farming, the USDA lent support, saying "a large number of farmers who operate small farms could change to organic farming with little economic impact on the U.S. economy."[62] In 1989, the National Academy of Sciences released a study that endorsed chemical-free farming. Their 17-member panel of experts stated that this approach can be as productive and even more profitable than conventional farming.[63]

In response to increasing demand, more companies are producing and selling organic foods. Sales reached $15 billion in 2004 and by 2006 about 67 percent of Americans said they "sometimes" or "often" bought organic foods, up from about 45 percent in 1989.[64] Conventional food producers often point out the higher cost of organics, but prices have declined overall as production increases and more stores sell organics. When Wal-Mart announced plans to double its organic food offerings in 2006, the company's CEO said, "We don't think you should have to have a lot of money to feed your family organic foods."[65]

Most consumers cite health benefits as their primary reason for buying organics.[66] In addition to safety factors, studies have shown that organic foods contain more nutrients, including antioxidants.[67] Tests conducted on organically and sustainably grown berries and corn have shown they contain up to 58 percent more polyphenolics (antioxidants that may protect cells against damage that can lead to cancer or heart disease) than conventional versions. Other researchers found that organic crops have significantly more vitamin C, iron, magnesium, and phosphorus, as well as lower amounts of some heavy metals.[68] In light of their benefits to consumers and the environment, supporters consider organic foods a bargain.

Summary

Since the 1940s, concerned people have worked to educate the public and strengthen laws regarding agricultural chemicals. More "average citizens" have joined these scientists, environmentalists, farm workers, and others calling for safer food. Other countries have recognized these dangers and decided to reduce pesticide use considerably. During the 1980s and 1990s, for example, Denmark, Sweden, and the Netherlands carried out successful plans to reduce their pesticide use by 50 percent.

In 2003, Carol Browner, who served as EPA administrator in the Clinton administration, told members of the American Wildlife Association:

> Agribusinesses that embraced the use of pesticides gave us farming practices that have begun to devastate the environment at levels still not fully understood or documented. . . . Common sense tells us that rather than pouring nearly 3 billion pounds of pesticides on our food—and then trying to wash them off, commission scientific studies about them [and] worry about how risky they might be—we ought to be figuring out how to use fewer pesticides in the first place.[69]

Regulatory agencies must critically examine each chemical they permit for food use, based on rigorous testing by independent scientists. They should strictly enforce laws to keep toxic chemicals out of the food supply and hold people accountable for breaking these laws. Even if some dangers cannot be proven beyond a doubt, it is foolish and unnecessary to take risks with human health. Alternatives to these chemicals offer the benefits of cleaner air, soil, and water, sounder ecosystems, and healthier farm workers and consumers.

Says one Missouri farmer who stopped using pesticides in 1979: "The label said to burn my work clothes afterward and I just decided I didn't want to be around anything that deadly."[70]

Using Approved Chemicals Is Safe and Offers Important Benefits

I n 1993, people who were worried about agricultural chemicals heard reassuring news. The U.S. Food and Drug Administration (FDA) concluded that pesticide residues in foods eaten by Americans were almost always below the amount permitted by the Environmental Protection Agency (EPA). During the course of a seven-year period, scientists at the Center for Food Safety and Applied Nutrition had analyzed findings on more than 10,000 samples of foods that infants and children tend to consume in large quantities: milk, apples, bananas, oranges, pears, and juice from apples, grapes, and oranges. The items they tested were neither washed nor peeled, and yet, fewer than 50 samples contained residues that exceeded allowable levels (0.3 percent of domestic products and 0.6 percent of imported products). They also found no pesticide residues in infant formulas. Since food processors and consumers usually wash and sometimes peel produce before eating, people are likely exposed to lower levels of these chemicals than the tests suggest.[71] Timothy Willard, a spokesperson for the National Food Processors Association, said this report was "in harmony with what the industry and scientists have said for years about food and health: that consumer and public health attention should focus on the real risks, rather than trivial and mostly hypothetical risks posed by synthetic or natural carcinogens."[72]

Four years earlier, in 1989, consumers had heard reports claiming that produce harbored dangerous chemicals. Several reports discussed Alar, a chemical used to keep apples from falling off the tree before they ripened. Growers noted that certain varieties of apples have weak bonds between the stem and tree branch. Without Alar, they fall to the ground before maturity. Dropped apples are sold for cider, meaning fewer fresh apples for consumers and less income for growers. To prevent such losses, some growers hired more pickers, leading to higher market prices. One orchard manager noted, "[Alar] gave us a longer

Natural Carcinogens

According to professor Anthony Trewavas, a research scientist at the Institute of Cell and Molecular Biology at the University of Edinburgh:

> Every day, each of us eats a quarter of a teaspoonful of carcinogens; 99.99 per cent of these are made naturally by all plants. . . . The remaining 0.01 per cent comes from food preparation and agricultural activities; in part these are carcinogens derived from the frying and smoking of food.

Source: Anthony Trewavas, "Is Organic Food Really Safe?" Monsanto Company, http://www .monsanto.co.uk/news/99/july99/300799_edinburgh.html.

time to harvest. Something that will keep the apple even one day longer on the tree can make a big difference."[73]

Following the Alar reports, scared consumers stopped buying apples, even though 85 to 95 percent of these fruits were not treated with the chemical. Prices fell to almost half of the break-even level. In Washington state alone, the USDA said growers lost at least $125 million in the six months after the initial reports. Farmers in New England, the Midwest, and other places also suffered; some lost their farms.[74]

Was Alar dangerous? People still disagree, and some say the research was inadequate. After studying this matter, Dr. Joseph D. Rosen, a professor of food science at Rutgers University, said, "There was never any legitimate scientific study to justify the Alar scare."[75] The California Department of Food and Agriculture and Britain's Advisory Committee on Pesticides both concluded that using Alar on apples in legally approved amounts posed only a negligible risk of cancer.

Although critics often lump all pesticides together as "dangerous," products approved for food use must meet strict government standards. Some, such as the synthetic fungicide Rubigan, have been declared nontoxic. Said one apple grower: "It's highly specific, it's biodegradable, it's benign, it has been released by the Environmental Protection Agency after 17 years of testing."[76] Critics also seem to ignore the fact that foods are themselves composed of chemicals. "About 6,000 chemicals, both synthetic and natural, are deliberately or inadvertently added to foods," author Jane Brody points out, "whereas hundreds of thousands of chemicals—perhaps a million—are naturally present in foods."[77]

Synthetic fertilizers and pesticides were developed for practical and compelling reasons: to increase crop yields, control ripening time, meet standards for quality and appearance, and prolong shelf life. These chemicals can eliminate pests, including insects that infest grains and dangerous funguses that can grow during production, storage, and shipping. As a result, Americans enjoy an array of reasonably priced foods year-round, even when they live far from places where foods are raised. Growers produce surplus crops for other countries, leading people to call the United States the "bread basket" of the world.

Critics who call agricultural chemicals unsafe and/or unnecessary may be overlooking scientific facts and the realities of global food production for an ever-growing population. Debates over these chemicals also cause dilemmas for consumers. As journalist Timothy Egan notes, "Faced with conflicting scientific reports, consumers are subject to 'scare of the week' stories by environmental groups and self-serving reports made by the chemical industry. . . ."[78]

Science has not proven that pesticides used in food production cause cancer; in fact, a diet high in fruits and vegetables offers health benefits.

People who support the use of synthetic pesticides say there is no conclusive proof that these products cause cancer or other diseases. In the past, some chemicals that appeared to be carcinogenic were banned. By 2000, the most controversial pesticides were no longer approved for use in food, and legal products had been rigorously tested. Besides, farmers rarely use every permissible chemical on a given crop; for example, they might use only 6 of 100 permissible chemicals. By the time foods reach consumers, pesticide residues are usually negligible and often undetectable. Washing reduces lingering pesticides and cooking can eliminate certain others.

Do pesticides cause cancer? Scientists offer studies and theories but no absolute proof. Humans are exposed to many health variables through their genetic makeup, diets, environments, and lifestyles, so these theories are difficult to prove. Scientists debate the conclusions and methodology of various studies, as well as the choices of test subjects. Referring to animal studies, Sandra Tirey of the Chemical Manufacturers Association (CMA) said, "We have to be careful about how we interpret these studies. There are differences between animal studies and human studies in terms of basic biology."[79]

Toxicologists have said that animal tests cannot predict actual risks for humans. Test animals receive large doses of chemicals and the tumors that grow in these animals may result from toxicity-related mechanisms, not a tumor-causing potential that is innate to the test chemical. Extremely high doses of chemicals can kill cells, which prompts an animal to produce new cells. Cells undergoing rapid growth are most vulnerable to cancerous changes. Dr. Bruce Ames, a biochemist at the University of California, Berkeley, suggests that using extremely high doses in cancer testing may help to explain why about 50 percent of the human-made and naturally occurring chemicals tested are regarded as mutagens and possible carcinogens.[80] Yet animal testing can show the relative risks of various chemicals, and that knowledge can help producers make optimal choices.[81]

Studies looking for links between cancers and human-made chemicals show conflicting results. In one study of American female farm and forestry workers, breast cancer rates were 84 percent below the national average.[82] In 1997, researchers who studied more than 32,000 women did not find higher levels of DDT and PCBs in women with breast cancer versus women who were cancer-free. Said Dr. David Hunter, associate professor of epidemiology and director of the Harvard Center for Cancer Prevention, "Smaller studies to date have been somewhat contradictory about whether there is a relationship between these chemicals and breast cancer risk. We observed no evidence of a positive association between organochlorine exposure and breast cancer risk."[83] Hunter also noted that DDT and PCBs are "found in virtually all people living in North America" but "do not appear to explain the high and increasing rates of breast cancer in the U.S."[84]

Furthermore, fruits and vegetables contain naturally occurring toxins and substances that may be carcinogenic in high amounts. Plants make these substances to protect themselves

Pesticides and fungicides can be essential to farmers; when certain conditions exist, an entire crop can be ruined by the ravages of insects or fungus. Above, a crop-dusting airplane is used to apply fungicide to a field of snap peas that were showing signs of white mold after excessive rainfall.

from diseases and animal and insect predators. Caffeic acid, a naturally occurring pesticide, is found in apples, lettuce, peaches, pears, potatoes, tomatoes, and citrus. Large amounts of caffeic acid have caused cancer in laboratory animals, but no links have been found between these foods and cancer in humans.[85] Scientists theorize that organic foods may have relatively more naturally occurring carcinogens because they are fighting pests without help from synthetic chemicals.[86]

Natural carcinogens in food outnumber synthetic ones, according to a 1996 report from the National Research Council, a branch of the National Academy of Sciences. People ingest larger amounts of these "natural pesticides"—perhaps 10,000 times more than human-made pesticides.[87] Scientists believe, however, that eating a variety of foods can prevent any one chemical from causing problems. The isoflavonoids, isothiocyanates, phenolic acids, and other cancer-fighting compounds in fruits and vegetables give added protection.

Foods contain other chemicals that might sound dangerous. For example, arsenic occurs in soil and tiny amounts can be found in some plants, including broccoli. Broccoli, however, a cruciferous vegetable, contains vitamin A, calcium, and fiber, along with cancer-fighting vitamin C, sulforaphane, indole, and isothiocyanates. Nutritionists rate broccoli as one of the healthiest foods around. When scientists at the World Cancer Research Fund reviewed 206 human and 22 animal studies, they found compelling evidence that cruciferous vegetables lower the risk for cancer of the uterus, lung, mouth, throat, stomach, esophagus, pancreas, and colon.[88] Numerous studies show the benefits of consuming several servings of fruits and vegetables daily.[89]

In 1996, the National Research Council released a 407-page report titled *Carcinogens and Anticarcinogens in the Human Diet*. After reviewing the scientific literature, this scientific panel said it could not conclude that human-made compounds are more toxic and carcinogenic than those that occur naturally in food. Nor did they reach the opposite conclusion. Instead, they stated, "Data are insufficient to determine whether the dietary cancer risks from naturally occurring substances exceed that for synthetic substances."[90]

Federal agencies and food safety laws protect consumers.

While nobody can guarantee that every food item is always 100 percent safe, food safety laws and regulatory agencies do protect the public. Government agencies work to ensure that pesticides and other farm chemicals are safe for use and are used according to the law. This process continues to improve, as laws and inspection procedures change to reflect new research, technology, and scientific techniques.

The EPA registers every pesticide sold or distributed in the United States, based on scientific studies showing that a given chemical will not pose unreasonable risks to people or the environment. "I've talked with a number of farmers across the country and I believe there's a way to grow our food with fewer chemicals," said Carol M. Browner, the director of the EPA during the Clinton administration (1993–2001). "I also think it's important that any chemical used on our food be required to meet a strict health and safety standard."[91]

Good Laboratory Standards

In 2001, the U.S. Food and Drug Administration Office of Regulatory Affairs issued this statement regarding its Good Laboratory Standards regulations:

The importance of nonclinical laboratory studies to FDA's public health decisions demands that they be conducted according to scientifically sound protocols and with meticulous attention to quality.

In the 1970s, FDA inspections of nonclinical laboratories revealed that some studies submitted in support of the safety of regulated products had not been conducted in accord with acceptable practice, and that accordingly data from such studies was not always of the quality and integrity to assure product safety. As a result of these findings, FDA promulgated the Good Laboratory Practice (GLP) Regulations, 21 CFR Part 58, on December 22, 1978 (43 FR 59986). The regulations became effective June 1979. The regulations establish standards for the conduct and reporting of nonclinical laboratory studies and are intended to assure the quality and integrity of safety data submitted to FDA.

Source: "Compliance Program Guidance Manual 7348.008 Part I—Background," FDA, http://www.fda.gov/ora/compliance_ref/bimo/7348_808/part_I.html.

Some experts find EPA standards quite stringent. Joseph D. Rosen, professor of food science at Rutgers University, writes:

> EPA guidelines mandate the use of extremely conservative mathematical models and exposure assumptions in order to err on the side of Safety: Thus the agency takes into account only the total number of benign and malignant tumors at the target site in the most sensitive species at very high doses. Data that indicate no danger are ignored. . . . As a result of its numerous conservative assumptions, this approach yields a risk assessment that is a worst-case scenario. Actual risk is much less and possibly nonexistent.[92]

From time to time, the EPA makes changes in light of new information or specific concerns. Worries about special vulnerabilities infants and children have to pesticides led to the Food Quality Protection Act of 1996. In that same year, the EPA began to review all pesticides approved before November 1, 1984, and considered whether each of them should be re-registered. The EPA took a closer look to ensure that the levels of residues on foods were safe for the very young. In people of all ages, the EPA has also been studying the impact of cumulative exposure to pesticide residues from all sources, and the cumulative effects of pesticides and other compounds.[93] As Congress ordered, the EPA began reviewing the 40,000 pesticides that had come onto the market without testing. It completed more than 90 percent of these reviews by 2006 and expects to finish the rest by 2008.

Critics complained when the Delaney clause was abandoned in 1996 in favor of the standard of "negligible risk," but many people noted problems with the clause. In a report for Congress in 1995, Donna U. Vogt, a life sciences analyst, pointed out:

> Delaney's standard of absolute zero or "no cancer-causing food additives" does not allow for the characterization of

relative risk in various foods, even if the risk of the residue is extremely small. The Delaney Clause's concept of zero risk inhibits the flexibility of a regulatory agency to make tolerance decisions based on the latest risk models because it means that even the most trivial risk cannot be allowed [and] creates a false expectation that a processed food will not have any cancer-causing substances in it. There are, however, many natural carcinogenic elements in foods to which humans are exposed. These natural toxins, such as fungi or aflatoxin, may be thousands of times more concentrated and potent than the residues from synthetic pesticides. . . . So when toxins are natural, the FDA cannot assume the responsibility of ensuring that foods will contain no cancer-causing substances.[94]

To fulfill its enforcement duties, the FDA checks for pesticide levels and examines foods in key settings: near the point of entry (imported foods), site of production, or site of distribution. The FDA routinely analyzes selected samples of specific foods. Using a method called Total Diet Study, the FDA studies data from supermarket shopping to analyze the contents of a typical diet and check for pesticide residues and other concerns. The agency also updates its testing methods with new scientific techniques.[95] It can take action when foods contain more than the allowed levels of pesticide residues. In addition, federal labeling laws help consumers stay informed by requiring companies to provide facts about packaged foods, including ingredients, nutritional content, and country of origin. The FDA also publishes educational materials about nutrition and food safety.[96]

Critics of the EPA and FDA may also be overlooking the financial and legal hurdles these agencies face. For one, chemical companies have sued the government to prevent them from canceling products. These cases, in addition to bureaucratic red tape, impede the process of banning products or removing them from use. Inadequate funding is a recurring problem as well. Under President Ronald Reagan, for example, budgets and staff were cut. By 1989, the FDA had only 1,000 inspectors and a $48 million budget. As more people demanded stricter enforcement, that budget was raised to $1.39 billion in 2001 and to $1.9 billion in 2006. But by then, the FDA had the additional job of carrying out a food antiterrorism program to keep the nation's food supply safe from sabotage during processing and packaging after 9/11.[97]

For their part, food producers have a strong interest in making sure their products are safe and legal. Recalls can cost millions of dollars and hurt a company's reputation. As a result, many companies conduct their own inspections and implement rigorous safety measures. Some food industry groups hire independent laboratories to test their products and certify them free of detectable pesticide residues. "We know our crop is safe," said one potato farmer in Maine. "Tests are not going to find anything. They are just going to verify what we've been saying all along."[98]

Pesticides and other chemicals can protect people from health hazards, including toxins and microbial contamination.

The 1988 U.S. corn crop contained high levels of a substance known to be a potent carcinogen in test animals. This substance was neither human-made nor something that was sprayed on plants; it was aflatoxin, produced by a fungus sometimes found in corn, peanuts, and cottonseed. Hot temperatures and other conditions caused it to grow in corn crops that year.

Aflatoxins are believed to be more carcinogenic than the fungicides people use against them. Aspergillus, the fungus that causes aflatoxin, belongs to a group of mycotoxins, which are both common and dangerous. According to the United Nations Food and Agriculture Organization, about 25 percent of the world's food crops are contaminated with mycotoxins.[99] Exposure to aflatoxins can cause liver damage, cancer of the liver and other organs, and gastrointestinal hemorrhages, among other problems. People and animals have died directly from eating moldy corn tainted with aflatoxin. Secondary poisoning from this fungus can also occur: When a cow eats contaminated feed, its milk carries the toxin, which can make its way into cheese and other dairy products.

Ergotism is caused by fungal alkaloids that can infect rye, wheat, or sorghum, a staple food in parts of Africa. These funguses produce toxic parasites, leading to hallucinations, severe intestinal distress, dry gangrene, and painful burning sensations.

Professor Anthony Trewavas, a research scientist at the Institute of Cell and Molecular Biology at the University of Edinburgh, says, "The use of effective fungicides has reduced the risk from mycotoxins in normal food, but not necessarily in organic food."[100] Pesticides can kill fungi directly, or indirectly by killing rodents and insects that bite plants, which provides openings for fungal growth.

Pesticides can also kill *E. coli,* salmonella, and other bacteria. Organic crops may be more vulnerable to bacteria because they are often fertilized with animal manure, regarded as a natural alternative to chemical fertilizers.[101] Manure that contains bacteria from the intestines of animals can cause diseases in humans. To kill bacteria, manure must be properly composted or dried and heated to a high enough temperature before use. Consumers have become ill and even developed chronic health problems after eating contaminated produce. In 1996, two children in Connecticut became ill after they ate triple-washed organic lettuce. One child was left with reduced kidney function and vision problems. In 2004, two outbreaks of food poisoning from *E. coli* involved organic lettuce and strawberries.[102]

Other alternatives to synthetic chemicals may be hazardous as well. For example, sulfur can kill pests but it may be contaminated with lead, a heavy metal that can endanger health. Some scientists are also concerned about insecticides made with bacterial spores, because studies show they can cause lung infections in mice and damage human cells in culture.[103]

The use of synthetic chemicals boosts the food supply while keeping food affordable, which improves nutrition and prevents hunger.

Modern farming methods have enabled developed nations to meet, and even exceed, their food needs, but some experts warn that crop output would decrease dramatically without synthetic pesticides and fertilizers. To those who advocate sustainable farming, former U.S. Secretary of Agriculture Earl Butz said, "Before we move in that direction, someone must decide which 50 million of our people will starve. We simply cannot feed, even at subsistence levels, our 250 million Americans without a large production input of chemicals, antibiotics, and growth hormones."[104] Journalist Steven Shapin writes, "According to a more recent estimate, if synthetic fertilizers suddenly disappeared from the face of the earth, about 2 billion people would perish."[105]

Food producers agree that synthetic chemicals are needed to grow enough food, and critics overlook the consequences of ending pesticide use. These consequences include problems with storing or shipping, so in wintertime, consumers might miss fruits and vegetables that grow only in warm climates. Eating produce enhances nutrition, and conventional produce costs less than organic, making healthy foods more affordable. Organic crops can suffer greater losses due to pests, and growing them can also require more labor; these are both conditions that prevailed before science and technology offered more efficient methods. Even farmers who support organic methods have said that the rigid requirements for organic farming are not pragmatic for large commercial food producers. In the past, farmers who stopped using chemicals reported problems selling produce with wormholes or blemishes, including streaks left by fungus growth. Fears over pesticides can also cause substantial economic losses to growers, as when people rejected apples and apple products after the Alar scare.

In addition, suitable alternatives to chemical fertilizers and pest controls sometimes simply aren't available. California and Florida growers were concerned in 1996 when the government banned the use of methyl bromide by 2001 because it seems to deplete Earth's ozone layer. This fumigant had been used to control bacteria, insects, and weeds on berries, grains, nuts, and other export crops. As of 1999, no effective substitute had been found, so the ban was delayed. The California Department of Food and Agriculture estimated that damaged crops would cause state growers losses of $346 million per year.[106] Smaller crop yields result in higher prices for consumers.

Are foods raised without pesticides more nutritious than conventionally raised foods? People disagree. "Some people mistakenly construe [organic food] to be safer or more nutritious, or even that it's entirely pesticide-free," says Tim Willard, president of the National Food Processors Association. "It's not."[107] The organic industry itself does not even claim that its products are more nutritious. Margaret Wittenberg of Whole Foods Markets was part of the board that helped to develop the organic labeling system. "The National Organic Standards Board has been very clear. Organic is a production method," she said.[108] The American Council on Science and Health, a nonprofit consumer advocacy organization, compared the nutritional content of conventional versus organic produce. It found similar vitamin contents, with a slightly higher vitamin C content for organic vegetables, amounting to 10 percent more of the recommended daily intake (RDA). Consumers could reach that RDA by adding an extra serving of fruit each day.[109]

Using synthetic chemicals can help the environment.

Cutting down forests is a serious environmental problem, causing the loss of wildlife habitat and contributing to global warming. Without synthetic chemicals, people would likely destroy more forests to grow crops, since using fertilizers and pesticides enables people to raise more crops on less land. Efficient conventional farming also releases land for animals and plants that cannot easily co-exist with agriculture, says scientist Anthony Trewavas.[110]

Population growth will require still larger yields in the future, so people must approach food production with a global perspective. "Given the way the world now is, sustainably grown and locally produced organic food is expensive," notes journalist Steven Shapin. "Genetically modified, industrially produced monocultural corn is what feeds the victims of an African famine, not the gorgeous organic technicolor Swiss chard from your local farmers' market."[111] Dennis T. Avery, author of *Saving the Planet With Pesticides and Plastic*, notes that in 2050, Asia "will be nine times more densely populated per acre of farmland as America."[112] Avery says that biological pest controls may be useful in some cases but will not likely replace chemical pest control; additionally, integrated pest management should not replace pesticides, but rather should be used to increase pesticide effectiveness. [113] As for fertilizer, he concludes, "Composting and organic fertilizer can only add marginally to our plant nutrient supply. Organic farmers cannot replace the huge supplies of chemical nitrogen and mined phosphate without clearing huge tracts of land for green manure crops."[114] (Green manure crops are plants sown close together in order to protect soil and to improve soil nitrogen content while fields are left to rest between regular crop plantings.)

People who oppose pesticide use often complain about soil erosion, but modern low-erosion techniques can reduce that problem. Dennis Avery quotes an agronomist who says that "for the first time in ten thousand years, people can grow crops without destroying the land."[115] Higher crop yields also mean that less land is subject to erosion. Pesticides kill insects that destroy foliage as well as crops, and lack of foliage makes

land more vulnerable to the effects of erosion. Some studies
show declining rates of soil erosion. When researcher Stanley W.
Trimble studied 140 years of data on sedimentation in a heavily farmed region in Wisconsin that drains into the Mississippi
River, he found that during recent decades, erosion rates there
seemed to be a tiny fraction of their historic highs.[116]

Summary

Throughout history, pests and plant diseases have caused mas-
sive crop destruction and even starvation. American homestead-
ers who went West suffered this crushing blow during the 1800s
when flying pests attacked and ate their new crops, which they
had labored so hard to grow. During the 1930s, locusts completely devastated farmland in the Dakotas, Colorado, Iowa, and
other states.

Then scientists developed products to aid food production,
resulting in unprecedented crop yields that provided whole-
some foods at affordable prices. The products and methods
spare farmers the backbreaking labor and losses that historically
plagued their predecessors. These products lengthen shelf life so
that produce can be shipped farther and stored longer and more
safely. By the time foods reach consumers, pesticide residues are
negligible or absent, but they have effectively killed pests, funguses, and bacteria that threaten human health.

No one has proven that synthetic pesticides cause cancer
or other diseases, and it is unnecessary and impractical to stop
using them. Such a decision could cause declining food production and other problems. Federal agencies do a good job of monitoring food-use chemicals; regulations are in place and they
are enforced. Products are rigorously tested. Although people
generally agree that chemicals should be regulated, decision-
makers should rely on solid scientific data that accurately shows

the risks. Dr. Joseph D. Rosen addressed these matters in "Much Ado About Alar," which appeared in a 1990 journal from the National Academy of Sciences.[117] Rosen stated, "Until we have some better way to weigh the risks of these things, there's always going to be another Alar scare."[118]

Genetically Modified Foods Can Be Dangerous for Consumers and the Environment

In 2000, people were startled to hear that a genetically modified (GM) type of corn, called StarLink, was turning up in tortillas, corn chips, and other foods. This corn was genetically modified to make a bacterium called Bt (for *Bacillus thuringiensis*) that kills corn borers and other pests. But government agencies decided that a protein in StarLink might cause allergic reactions in some people, so in 1998, the EPA approved it for use only in animal feed. Still, somehow this corn had reached the human food supply.

The problem surfaced that fall after dozens of Americans developed allergic reactions, some quite severe, shortly after eating corn products.[119] Testing showed that StarLink corn was present in these foods, so all products that might be affected were removed from markets as a precaution. It was later determined that pollen from these corn plants had reached neighboring areas where StarLink grew among conventional corn crops. Some farmers were growing GM corn without even realizing it.

In 2006, trace amounts of an unapproved strain of GM rice were found in fields of commercial rice growing in the southeastern United States. Farmers filed a lawsuit against the company that bred this rice, saying that it breached its duty to prevent these seeds from contaminating other crops. That same year, farm workers in Texas developed blisters on their arms after harvesting a kind of celery that was genetically designed to resist certain diseases. This celery was producing a chemical that caused skin reactions—something its producers had not predicted.[120]

The examples above show some problems that can occur with genetically modified plants and the challenges of controlling how and where they are grown and used. This is why many people have questioned the safety and relative value of these foods.

Different terms are used to refer to the process of changing the genes in a plant or other organism; these terms include *modify, engineer, recombine,* and *manipulate.* The term *transgenic* is often used to describe GM foods, since this indicates that a crop contains genes from more than one entity. Crops may be engineered to prevent them from dying when herbicides are used on the weeds around them, or to improve shelf life, appearance, or texture.

Genes carry coded information that "tells" an organism how to make proteins that combine with other proteins. These processes are complex and specific. In nature, genes rarely cross between unlike species, and if they do, the offspring of the two species are sterile, unable to have offspring of their own. But through genetic engineering, scientists can isolate and remove a gene or piece of DNA from one source and paste that into another source—for example, moving a gene from a fish into a vegetable.

To create a GM food, scientists insert several materials into the host: a foreign gene, vector (material that carries the gene), promoter (substance that helps the host plant accept the new gene), and a marker that shows them the gene has reached its target. In most cases, the vectors are viruses. These viruses attack the cells of the host, or recipient, in order to deliver the new DNA into that organism. Many of the foreign genes come from bacteria, and many promoters are viruses. Promoters allow the new gene to express itself—to make the protein it is intended to make. These new combinations of DNA give the cells new instructions that create a modified plant.

A type of canola oil was an early GM product, and GM tomatoes were launched in 1994. By 2007, the list of GM foods included soybeans, corn, cotton, squash, eggplant, cabbage, lettuce, potatoes, celery, and others. Between 1996 and 2002, the amount of acreage devoted to GM seeds went from a few million worldwide to more than 120 million.[121] Most of this acreage was in the United States (68 percent), with Argentina second (22 percent).[122]

Does New Technology Always Mean "Progress"?

Going beyond politics and safety issues, critics see other dangers in genetic engineering. Says author and farmer Brewster Kneen:

> The lack of respect for the amazingly complex world of life we are born into, coupled with a belief in progress achieved through ever more powerful technologies, breeds a profound dissatisfaction with life as it is. This in turn drives a relentless quest to improve on life, while *hubris* arms us with the assurance that we can do no harm, and if we do make mistakes, we will soon find another technological fix for them.

Source: Brewster Kneen, *Farmegaddon: Food and the Culture of Biotechnology* (Gabriola Island, B.C., Canada: New Society Publishers, 1999), 7–8.

By 2005, GM plants occupied an estimated 222 million acres.[123] More than half of all GM crops were being grown in the United States, with the rest grown in 20 other countries.

The impact of this technology is widespread, and many people eat GM foods without knowing it. Aside from StarLink, certain types of GM corn have been approved for human consumption. Some contain a Bt gene while others are engineered to survive weed killers. GM corn made up about 25 percent of the U.S. corn crop in 2001.[124] Corn is used for corn syrup and corn oil, which in turn are used in snacks, cereals, soft drinks, and many other foods. Since corn products and soy products appear in so many common foods, an estimated 60 to 70 percent of the processed foods in U.S. supermarkets contain GM ingredients.[125]

Proponents of GM foods say they offer benefits in terms of appearance, taste, and nutrition and can help the environment and reduce hunger around the world. Critics disagree. These critics include scientists, environmentalists, ethicists, consumers, and diverse organizations such as Greenpeace, Christian Aid, Friends of the Earth, and the Institute for Food and Development Policy. In 1998, the European Union (EU) banned GM crops from EU nations and announced that such crops would not be imported.

Critics say that genetically modifying foods poses health risks and can exacerbate environmental problems and world hunger. Some scientists, people who began studying this field with an open mind, have by now developed reservations. Molecular biologist Margaret Mellon, director of the food and environment program of the Union of Concerned Scientists, says that she "was initially more positively disposed toward biotechnology" but changed her viewpoint over the years as she asked questions and learned more about the technology.[126]

Longtime consumer advocate Ralph Nader speaks for many critics when he says that genetic engineering techniques have advanced faster than the science relating to ecology, the dynamics of nutrition and disease, and basic molecular genetics.[127] The risks seem to outweigh the benefits; the world does not really need GM foods, and besides that, there are safer alternatives.

GM foods are not just an extension of traditional breeding.

Supporters of GM foods often say that genetic modification is an extension of traditional plant breeding practices. But these older practices, such as the grafting of one apple tree to another, observed nature itself and took advantage of changes that occur on their own. This was the case even when people bred a domestic crop with a wild relative to make it hardier, tastier, or more nutritious. Unlike genetic engineering, traditional plant breeding respects the complex, sometimes mysterious, workings of nature. As authors Martin Teitel and Kimberly A. Wilson write, "By relying on the birds and bees rather than the microscope and Petri dish to determine the success or failure of new crops, classical plant breeders take advantage of nature's vast storehouse of information, accumulated over millions of years of experimentation, as to what works."[128]

In genetic engineering, scientists go beyond traditional breeding or the crossbreeding that occurs in nature and they combine genes in ways that would never be found in existing organisms—not just crosses of species, but crosses of organisms from different kingdoms. Critics have expressed grave concern about foods that contain genetic material from species that would not normally crossbreed or interbreed. For these and other reasons, GM techniques entail more risks than traditional breeding. The impact is unpredictable.

The safety of GM foods is not fully known, so it must be considered whether they are potentially hazardous.

Scientists note that DNA is unstable once it is taken from its customary environment, so the transplantation of genes can have unpredictable effects on physiology and biochemistry. Most genes work in combination with other genes rather than alone to cause a specific trait, and genes continue to actively interact with each other and the environment after being recombined. Molecular geneticist Michael Antoniou points out that it is not the "artificial nature" of GM crops that makes them dangerous, but rather "it is the imprecise way in which genes are combined and the unpredictability in how the foreign gene will behave in the new host that results in uncertainty."[129]

These unknowns could cause hazards in the foods themselves. For instance, transplanted genes could trigger the production of toxins or allergens. Plants already contain numerous toxins; manipulating their genetic structure might cause them to make larger amounts. Changing a plant's normal functioning might also make it less nutritious. Food producers would not want to purposely make an unsafe or inferior food, but the fact is that they do not fully understand the systems they are altering. No one does.

Other risks arise because viral material is inserted, especially in the case of the promoters. Critics fear the viruses could activate dormant viruses in the host or combine with active viruses, causing unforeseen results. Mae-Wan Ho, a geneticist and biophysicist, has expressed specific concerns about using the 35S promoter, which drives genes when cauliflower mosaic virus, a powerful promoter, is present. The use of 35S in GM foods has been patented since the 1980s. Scientists note that in the cauliflower plant family, this virus is encased in protein so it does not infect humans, but when the version called 35S is placed in plants, that protein coat is gone. Mae-Won Ho called the use of 35S in transgenic plants a "recipe for disaster."[130] She warned that it might spark activity from undesirable genes, including those that cause cancer, and called biotechnology in general "crude, unreliable, and unpredictable."[131]

Some scientists say the greatest risk involves the conversion of nonallergenic foods to allergens. Researchers mix genes from various species, including plants that people usually don't eat.

Problems can arise, however, even when scientists use well-known plants. During the 1990s, genetic researchers made a soybean using a protein from the Brazil nut. Nuts can cause severe allergic reactions, and testing showed that this new soybean had that capability, too, so it was abandoned. If products with this potential do reach the marketplace, people who develop allergic symptoms may not understand why, or know which foods to avoid.

Another potential hazard involves spreading antibiotic resistance in disease-causing bacteria. Antibiotic marker genes are often used in genetic engineering. If resistance develops and those genes move from GM foods to bacteria inside the person's digestive tract, he or she could develop resistance to antibiotics that are used to fight infectious diseases. Most companies have recognized this pitfall and have stopped using antibiotic-resistant genes.

FROM THE BENCH

Diamond v. Chakrabarty, **447 U.S. 303 (1980)**

In 1980, the U.S. Supreme Court was asked to decide whether living cells can be patented under Title 35 U.S.C. 101, which provides for the issuance of a patent to a person who "invents or discovers any new and useful manufacture or composition of matter." In the past, patent protection had been extended to new varieties of plants but not bacteria. Ananda Mohan Chakrabarty, a genetic engineer for General Electric, sought a patent after he developed a genetically engineered bacterium that could break down crude oil, making it useful for dealing with oil spills.

The court noted that this bacterium had a trait that "is possessed by no naturally occurring bacteria" and wrote: "A live, human-made micro-organism is patentable subject matter under 101. Respondent's micro-organism constitutes a 'manufacture' or 'composition of matter' within that statute." The court's decision in this case has been used to support the idea that someone can own the patent rights to a living organism.

Since scientists cannot yet accurately predict how engineered entities might affect those that already exist, many experiments with GM foods are considered failures. Author Kathleen Hart cites some untoward effects that have occurred in experiments with animals: ". . . a single gene that enhances the production of growth hormone was inserted into various farm animals with the hopes of making them grow faster. The inserted gene gave sheep diabetes and made them die young. . . . In pigs the elevated levels of growth hormone caused arthritis, stomach ulcers, and heart and skin abnormalities."[132]

Agencies set up to oversee food safety can do more to guarantee safety and inform consumers.

Regulations governing GM foods are too permissive; these foods should be more strictly examined. The responsibility for overseeing GM foods is divided among various agencies: The USDA regulates field testing for crops, the EPA regulates those crops that are bioengineered to make their own pesticides, and the FDA is supposed to make sure crops are safe for consumption.

The FDA, however, has decided that no new or special regulations are needed to deal with GM foods. This decision is based on the idea that GM foods do not differ substantially from conventional versions either in form or nutritional value. The FDA does not ban companies from using potentially allergenic genetic material or require labeling of these items, nor has it banned the use of antibiotic markers. Critics say that few careful, peer-reviewed studies have been conducted comparing GM food to non-GM food. Most testing is done on animals, not people, so scientists cannot know all the possible effects in humans, especially over a long period of time.

The companies themselves test GM foods, and they have a vested interest in selling their products. Sales of GM food products can also boost sales of related products. As one example, critics cite the Monsanto Company's widely sold Roundup Ready soybean. This plant was designed to withstand intensive herbicide spraying, a strength that would enable farmers to kill weeds without harming crops. About 85 percent of all cropland in the United States is treated with herbicides. Sales of Roundup Ready beans have, in turn, increased sales of the company's herbicide, Roundup, which is used on GM soybeans and corn sold by Monsanto.[133]

No regulations require markets or restaurants to label GM foods as such. Critics attribute this lack of regulation to lobbying efforts by the powerful food industry. In the case of GM soybeans, for example, companies say it would be too costly and impractical to separate them from conventional soybeans. Companies also argue that consumers have unreasonable fears about GM foods and labeling them as such would arouse more unnecessary concerns.[134]

Since large corporations are primarily concerned with profits, government agencies must be even more careful to set standards and provide supervision. At the very least, consumers have the right to know what they are eating.

Genetic engineering does not help the environment, and can even harm it.

GM proponents say that GM agriculture helps the environment in several ways, but this is subject to debate. Producing crops that resist the killing effects of herbicides encourages the use of more chemicals to kill weeds, which, in turn, harms the environment. When the USDA conducted studies to see if farmers growing Bt corn had reduced their use of pesticides, it found no significant change, even though the Bt corn had been developed to create its own pesticide.[135]

Although farmers raising Bt cotton did reduce their pesticide use, scientists wonder how long the Bt trait will remain effective. Pests are likely to become resistant, so the protective genetic traits in these plants will stop working against them at some point. As pests, molds, and other conditions attack GM plants, scientists will be forced to develop new plants that resist pests and disease until they, too, lose those capabilities. This vicious cycle will not produce solid or lasting environmental gains.

GM plants also affect the environment when genes move from engineered plants to their relatives growing in nearby fields or the wild. The lab is a controlled setting; in the outdoors, wind and insects can carry away pollen from GM plants. Once these genes reach other areas or plants, their effects can be difficult or impossible to control. Jumping genes, as they are called, can create new toxins and allergens or kill beneficial insects or species. In 2001, for example, environmentalists complained that pollen from GM corn was killing the larvae of monarch butterflies.

Jumping genes also might create out-of-control, invasive "superweeds." "Widespread use of GM crops has already led to the creation of herbicide-resistant weeds in Canada and the U.S.," Dr. Margaret Mellon points out.[136] In 2006, EPA investigators discovered an outbreak of a wild GM crop in Oregon after GM grass genes moved into wild grasses. Some were located more than two miles away from the site of the GM turf that was being test-grown. Although this grass might not harm people, scientists worry about what could happen if genes from plants being engineered to make pharmaceuticals were to escape and move into food crops.

Another environmental problem associated with GM crops is the decline of biodiversity, a side effect of too much land being devoted to fewer crops. This can also occur if GM traits invade other crops. In nature, plants develop mechanisms to survive under various conditions, such as climate changes. Diversity is important for growth and reproduction, environmental adaptations, and genetic material. As crops interact with their environments, diversity helps them to survive. Raising a limited number of crops can be disastrous, because if a disease hits a field that is only planted with one kind of crop, the entire harvest is wiped out. This happened in Ireland during the potato famine of the mid-1800s. Irish peasants subsisted heavily on a certain type of potato that was vulnerable to potato blight. When spores of the disease reached Ireland, whole fields of potatoes rotted, literally overnight.

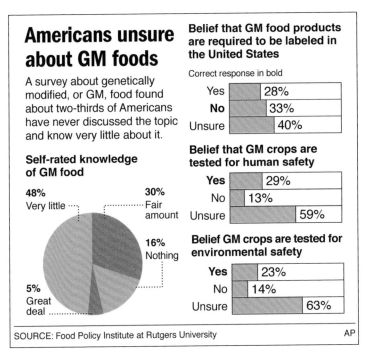

Americans unsure about GM foods

A survey about genetically modified, or GM, food found about two-thirds of Americans have never discussed the topic and know very little about it.

Self-rated knowledge of GM food

48% Very little

30% Fair amount

16% Nothing

5% Great deal

Belief that GM food products are required to be labeled in the United States

Correct response in bold

Yes	28%
No	33%
Unsure	40%

Belief that GM crops are tested for human safety

Yes	29%
No	13%
Unsure	59%

Belief GM crops are tested for environmental safety

Yes	23%
No	14%
Unsure	63%

SOURCE: Food Policy Institute at Rutgers University · · · · · · · · · · · · · · · · · · · AP

Genetic modification of food is still a relatively unknown process in the United States. A 2005 Food Policy Institute poll showed that about two-thirds of American had never discussed the topic and knew very little about it, as illustrated in the graphics above.

These environmental concerns also extend to genetic engineering of animals used for food, such as livestock and fish. Critics worry that GM fish, for example, could alter native ecosystems and even drive wild species to extinction.

GM is not an effective solution for world hunger or malnutrition, and might even worsen those problems.

As of 2007, more than 800,000 people around the world were either suffering from hunger or were malnourished. Supporters of GM foods say the technology can improve this situation by increasing crop yields on smaller areas of land, providing more nutrient-dense foods, and developing plants that grow under adverse conditions, such as drought. Critics say these arguments are flawed and do not address the root causes of hunger, which include politics, economics, cultural differences, local customs, and growing conditions. Many experts say there is already enough food to feed the world's people, but those who need it don't always get it or cannot afford to buy it. Some countries, such as the United States, have more than enough food per person.

Furthermore, companies that spend millions of dollars developing GM products would aim to profit from their investment, and they earn more money selling products to affluent consumers rather than those in developing nations. "Like all industries, this one serves investors who demand rapid returns, and financial considerations inevitably influence decisions related to product development," author Marion Nestle points out.[137]

Studies also challenge the assertion that GM foods provide higher yields. Crop yields differ depending on many factors, including climate, soil, and the region. Studies at the University of Nebraska, for example, showed that Roundup Ready soybeans gave a slightly lower number of bushels per acre than non-GM plants.[138] In addition, farming methods used in developed nations do not automatically work in parts of Africa, Asia, or Latin America, where people face harsh growing conditions including drought and lack of modern equipment.

GM also continues the trend of putting food control into fewer hands. For centuries, farmers have selected, saved, and traded the seeds of crops they planned to grow. As agriculture became big business after the 1930s, growers became increasingly dependent on seed companies. These and other developments brought increased centralization of the global food supply. Under current laws, companies can acquire plant genes from any region or country and then apply for patents on the GM crops they develop from these genes. The terms *bioprospecting* and *biopiracy* refer to the process of hunting for exotic genes in undeveloped countries and then using them to patent new crops.

New laws have helped corporations gain even further control. Companies can patent both their GM product and the process involved in making it. For example, after Monsanto Company set out to increase the levels of beta-carotene in rapeseed for canola oil, the company received a patent that covered "a transgenic plant which produces seed having altered carotenoid levels."[139] This could apply to other plants beside rapeseed. Critics consider patent rights such as these far too broad. In 1996, a coalition of concerned citizens petitioned Congress "to protect our common living heritage" with laws that will "exclude living organisms and their component parts from the patent system."[140]

Agribusinesses can even program plants to kill their own seeds at the end of the growing season. Called "terminator" technology, these methods threaten the ability of farmers to save seeds for the next year's crops. In addition, wind and insects can carry these sterile seeds to other areas, causing sterility in more plants. Critics have petitioned the USDA and various state governments to ban this practice, but the laws have not changed. In response to public concerns, Monsanto announced in 1999 that it would not commercialize the sterile seed technology known as "terminator," and some other companies and university science departments have made similar announcements.

Even when new crops could improve nutrition, they still might not be used for the clear benefit of humankind. During the late 1990s, a new rice containing beta-carotene was produced with the help of public research funds. Beta-carotene is needed to produce vitamin A, an important nutrient. Lack of vitamin A can cause blindness and other health problems, so this crop could potentially improve nutrition in places where rice is a staple food. Biotech companies praised this "golden rice" as an example of how GM foods help people.

As scientists discussed ways to bring golden rice to malnourished people, however, legal issues arose. Attorneys found that 70 patents relating to 32 different crops might need to be addressed before this rice could be given free to farmers. For example, there were patents on daffodil genes and a bacterium that had been used to make the rice. "Golden rice was a disturbing example of just how close the seed conglomerates had come through international patents to owning every step of the process of taking a gene from one plant and inserting it into another, as well as the transgenic product containing the alien gene," author Peter Pringle points out.[141]

Analysts also wondered how methods of processing, storing, and cooking the rice would affect nutrients. They estimated that people would need to eat pounds of this rice per day to obtain enough beta-carotene. People also need to consume a certain amount of fat to take advantage of vitamin A, a fat-soluble vitamin, and many poor people in developing countries lack adequate dietary fat. Cultural issues would likely arise, too, since

FDA Background Paper: Biotechnology of Food

In 1994, the FDA explained its policies for approving bioengineered food, specifically the first GM tomatoes to be approved for consumption:

The law places a responsibility on producers and sellers to offer only safe products to consumers, and provides FDA with the legal tools for enforcement.

Food law requires pre-market approval for food additives, whether or not they are the products of biotechnology. Therefore, FDA's biotechnology policy treats substances intentionally added to food through genetic engineering as food additives if they are significantly different in structure, function, or amount than substances currently found in food. Many of the food crops currently being developed using biotechnology do not contain substances that are significantly different from those already in the diet and thus do not require pre-market approval.

Source: U.S. Food and Drug Administration, Center for Food Safety and Applied Nutrition, "Biotechnology of Food," May 18, 1994, http://www.cfsan.fda.gov/~lrd/biotechn.html.

some people value white rice for its color and/or religious significance. They might have to be convinced to eat golden rice.

Author and scientist Vandana Shiva has criticized the value of GM technology in the fight against hunger and malnutrition. She claims that the agriculture business has harmed nutritious fruit and vegetable crops that people have cultivated for many years. For example, herbicides used on Western varieties of wheat nearly caused bathua, a vitamin A–rich, leafy vegetable grown in northern India, to become extinct. Says Shiva, "Instead of millions of farmers breeding and growing thousands of crop varieties to adapt to diverse ecosystems and diverse food systems, the Green Revolution reduced agriculture to a few varieties of a few crops (mainly rice, wheat, and maize) bred in one centralized research center in the Philippines for rice and Mexico for wheat and maize."[142]

GM plants can only make a real difference if governments, industry, and special interest groups do not prevent these foods from reaching those in need. But no food, however promising, can fix poverty, poor public health, sanitation problems, and other causes of hunger and malnutrition. Wars, dictators, lack of money to buy food, and other factors must be addressed.

Individuals also need practical solutions, including education and home gardens for growing their own crops. In India, for example, educators have used the radio and schools to teach people these techniques. Other promising solutions include changes in trade policies, land reform, and improving the infrastructure in countries where food does not reach hungry people. Focusing on GM as a solution distracts policymakers from the real problems.

GM foods are neither necessary nor desirable, considering the potential risks.

Do people really need GM foods? Critics say no. American consumers can already choose from more than 300,000 food products, with thousands of new ones added each year. Many people doubt the supposed benefits of GM foods, since they do not look or taste better than non-GM foods. They do not cost less and they do not offer enough nutritional benefits to make them a safe, reliable alternative.

Growers themselves have said they have enough seeds for food production without GM varieties. A farmer in Washington state comments, "There are 10,000 natural varieties of soybeans—plenty to choose from—we simply don't need a genetic mutation of an already exceptional selection."[143]

Considering the dubious benefits of GM foods, the risks of growing and consuming them seem unreasonable. In comparing genetic engineering of foods versus drugs, Dr. Margaret Mellon notes, "The therapeutic benefits of the new drugs outweigh the risks, and often there aren't any alternatives. But in agriculture, it's different. So far, at least, there are only modest benefits associated with biotechnology products, and it has yet to be shown that the benefits outweigh the risks. And there are exciting alternatives to solving agricultural problems that we are simply ignoring."[144]

Summary

Scientists and corporations have given themselves the power to change the very instructions that govern life—instructions that have been evolving slowly and naturally since life began on this planet. Meddling in these matters requires extraordinary care to prevent undesirable effects on society and the environment. GM foods have not delivered the nutritional and other benefits their proponents promised, nor have they alleviated world hunger and malnutrition. On the contrary, research and development of these products appears to be largely focused on profits, like other commercial enterprises.

When food is involved, decisions affect everyone and require proof of safety, not just theories or good intentions.

Experimental foods could affect billions of people and the planet in general, which places a huge burden of proof of safety on food producers. Since nobody knows the long-term consequences of GM foods, this technology should move forward slowly and with caution. As one group of scientists said in 2006, "We urge you to stop feeding the products of this infant science to our population and ban the release of these crops into the environment where they can never be recalled."[145]

Genetically Modified Foods Are Safe for Consumption and Have Other Advantages

More than one-third of the world's population eats rice as its primary food, and many of these people live in places where hunger and malnutrition are widespread. Since the 1980s, the Rockefeller Foundation and other institutions have funded a project that aims to boost the nutritional benefits of rice through biotechnology.[146] In 1999, German researchers found a way to produce rice that contains the essential nutrient beta-carotene. Dr. Ingo Potrykus and Dr. Peter Beyer, who developed this rice, knew that beta-carotene was present in the leaves and husk of rice, but not in the grain itself. Using a gene from the dandelion plant and a bacterium, they found a way to induce rice plants to develop with beta-carotene within their grains.

Critics of GM foods complain that bioengineering is done to benefit growers, food products companies, and seed merchants only. But in fact, the scientists and the Swiss crop protection company Syngenta donated their rice product for humanitarian use in developing countries. These researchers have worked on improvements that add still more nutrients to the rice.

The idea of genetically changing plants and animals is not new. Scientists were already working on these techniques in the 1960s, but it took them several decades to produce the first GM tomatoes, which reached supermarkets and made headlines in autumn 1993. Researchers had found ways to alter the tomato plants in order to extend their shelf life and maintain their taste and texture during long distance travel to markets. Using genetic engineering techniques, scientists at several research companies produced new brands. In southern New Jersey, DNA Plant Technologies Inc. (DNAP) developed a biogenetic process that it patented under the name Transwitch. This process suppresses the gene that causes a tomato to ripen, which means that it can remain on the vine longer to develop its distinctive flavor without becoming overripe. In California, researchers at Calgene Inc. developed their version of a gene-spliced tomato, also by finding a way to block the gene that causes tomatoes to soften and then rot.

Since 1993, corn, soybeans, rice, potatoes, papaya, and other plants have been genetically modified. Crops might be modified in order to extend shelf life, improve taste, prevent diseases, or improve resistance to insects and other pests. Scientists also seek ways to make a plant more productive—for example, canola plants that produce more oil. With the approval of government agencies, various genetically engineered foods have been cultivated and brought onto the market.

Despite these successes, GM foods have been attacked from the outset by consumer and environmental groups, including the international organization Greenpeace and the Pure Food Campaign, based in Washington, D.C. Most critics protest verbally, in the media, or through peaceful demonstrations, but others have tried to physically prevent GM research. In 1999, for example, opponents attacked fields in Britain, digging up and destroying GM crops. Consumer groups also have organized boycotts of GM foods and stores that sell them.

Some critics have been known to base their opinions on inadequate information or misconceptions, failing to understand the scientific processes involved in GM foods. An anti-science bias seems to drive some people who oppose, on principle, the idea of using *any* methods that seem to tamper with nature. During a 1999 interview, Alan Kerr, professor emeritus of plant pathology and recipient of the Australia Prize, noted that opponents to genetically engineered crops often raise three points: mad cow disease in Britain, the Chernobyl nuclear disaster in the former Soviet Union, and the dioxin contamination of chicken feed that occurred in Belgium during the late 1990s. But as Kerr pointed out, "None of these has anything to do with genetic engineering."[147] Fear of the unknown also seems to play a role when people argue against the production, marketing, and consumption of GM foods. These arguments ignore the social, economic, and nutritional benefits of foods produced through genetic engineering.

GM foods can offer superior taste, quality, and longevity, as well as more nutrients.

Agricultural biotechnology can benefit growers, retailers, and consumers alike. Genetically engineered tomatoes, for example, can be vine-ripened year-round. This adds longevity and creates more appealing produce, since consumers prefer the taste of vine-ripened tomatoes to that of artificially ripened tomatoes. In order to ship tomatoes out of season, growers typically pick them while they are green and not yet ripe. About 80 percent of these tomatoes are then treated with ethylene gas to make them turn red. GM tomatoes stay firm for two weeks after they are picked ripe, so they can be shipped (from Florida to Boston, for instance) and then sold with one to three days remaining in their shelf life.

Genetic engineering can improve other attributes, too, including freezing qualities and consistency. Scientists have worked on gene-splicing techniques to produce ice cream that resists the formation of ice crystals. They also hope to make strawberries that will not turn as mushy in the freezer. New brands of potatoes would feature less starch and water, which means they would absorb less fat when fried, resulting in a healthier dish. These traits—longer shelf life, better shipping properties, and improved appearance, taste, and texture—make produce more appealing, which can encourage people to eat more of these foods. Fruits and vegetables tend to be high in fiber, vitamins, cancer-fighting antioxidants, and other nutrients, so they are vital to a healthy diet.

Genetic modification can produce foods with new nutritional benefits or the ability to grow better in poor conditions. Nutrient-dense staple foods can help reduce malnutrition in regions where people lack access to a varied diet. For example, rice has been cultivated for more than 10,000 years and is the world's most important food crop, and because of this it is a valuable tool to administer vitamin boosts. Genetically modified golden rice contains beta-carotene, which is found in yellow and orange vegetables, such as yams and carrots. Beta-carotene is a precursor of vitamin A, which people need for healthy eyesight and an effective immune system. Golden rice would be especially useful in regions plagued by drought, since people have trouble growing other vegetables in dry climates. This could improve nutrition in Asia and other places where children who grow up eating a diet primarily made up of rice have higher rates of premature death and blindness. As of 2006, the World Health Organization estimated that between 250,000 and 500,000 children were going blind each year due to vitamin A deficiency.[148] A weaker immune system also means they cannot fight off infections effectively.

Genetic engineering expands upon techniques that have been used for decades and is not "unnatural," since genetic changes occur in nature, too.

Genetically modified plants are cultivated using techniques that have existed for many years, such as cross-fertilization, in which plant breeders combine the traits of more than one plant. Cross-fertilization is a form of genetic manipulation. It has resulted in many useful plants, including hybrid sweet corn, a cucumber with a yellow-orange color that contains more beta-carotene than traditional cucumbers, and potatoes that resist a disease called blight. Some plant breeders also use a technique called somoclonal variation, which takes advantage of the genetic changes that occur spontaneously in plants.

Newer techniques of plant modification involve gene-splicing and recombinant DNA (that is, DNA that has been made by combining the genetic codes of different organisms). With standard crossbreeding, hundreds or even thousands of genes are introduced into a plant at one time. Biotechnology allows scientists to change living cells in far more specific ways than cross-fertilization. They can target a specific trait and change a plant's genetic makeup accordingly, without adding other traits that might be undesirable. Scientists can also use genetic material from other kinds of organisms—for example, bacteria and animals—to improve varieties of plants.

Genetic changes occur in nature, and ideas for improving plants can come from studying diseases that cause destructive changes in plant DNA. Dr. Alan Kerr made use of such knowledge during the 1960s when he and other scientists were studying the agrobacterium, which lives in soil and causes crown gall. This bacterial disease attacks stone fruit trees, including almond, cherry, and peach, causing extensive damage as large tumor-like structures called galls form around their upper branches and leaves (called the crown). Scientists noticed that even after the bacteria were killed, galls continued to grow on the plants. They learned that these agrobacteria transmit their own genetic material into the plant cells, which then grow like a cancer. This bacterial DNA "instructs" the plant to make certain nutrients that agrobacteria need to survive. In effect, the plant is genetically altered—and seriously damaged—by a naturally occurring microorganism.

Further research showed that the bacterial DNA caused the plants to produce two hormones: auxin and cytokinin, which led to the formation of the galls. Scientists found a way to remove the specific genes in the bacterial DNA and substitute DNA from another organism. By 1983, they had produced such a GM plant.[149] This kind of research presents opportunities to replace the genetic material in plants with useful genes that can help plants fight diseases or resist pests.

GM foods are not dangerous, and those that do endanger consumers or the environment can be banned.

Are GM foods dangerous, as some critics claim? There is no proof that genetic engineering per se poses a health threat. Government policies and regulations, scientific ethics, and commercial considerations aim to prevent the production and sale of foods that would cause harm. A plant or other food item would be toxic for consumers if it contained genes that produce toxins, but such items have no commercial or food value, so researchers and food producers have no reason to develop or raise them. Foods that might trigger allergic reactions in certain people can be kept off the market or labeled in ways that protect the public.

Along with the scientific ethics that govern researchers, regulatory boards and agencies oversee these products. In the United States, the Food and Drug Administration (FDA) has developed sound policies toward genetically modified foods.

The FDA stated in May 1992 that it planned to regulate GM foods in the same ways that it regulates other foods. The agency stated its position this way:

> FDA's policy for genetically engineered foods covers all foods produced from new plant varieties developed by any method of plant breeding. The policy is based on the Food, Drug, and Cosmetic Act's requirements of post-market surveillance of foods and pre-market approval of new substances. This system has ensured the safety of foods and food additives for many years.[150]

FDA regulations require testing when any given food raises safety concerns. They also require labels on foods that are significantly changed from their original form or have characteristics much different from what consumers expect—for example, an orange without vitamin C. This reflects the FDA policy of requiring labels that contain "material information" about a product. Brad Stone, a spokesman for the FDA, said that GM foods would not receive special scrutiny unless a compelling safety issue exists.[151]

The FDA has been cautious. For example, it conducted four years of tests before approving GM tomatoes for consumption. It tested them for toxins, nutritional value, fungal resistance, and other traits. The FDA has also issued guidelines to companies that produce GM foods, informing them of what kind of tests are required to meet agency standards. Among other things, companies must test for potential toxins, nutrients, unexpected effects, and the potential to cause antibiotic resistance in consumers.

The FDA reports that companies have cooperated in conducting these tests and have sought agency guidance while testing products before seeking approval to bring them onto the market.[152] Manufacturers seeking approval for a product submit test results to the FDA. These tests compare the chemical structure and nutrient contents of the GM version of the food with the conventional version. Extensive allergy testing is done to determine whether the proteins produced by the inserted genes cause toxic reactions in animals when given in high amounts. In addition, manufacturers refrain from using genes from sources with a high risk of allergy, such as peanut genes.

Should the government require labels that show when foods contain a GM ingredient? The FDA does not require such labeling, except in cases when a product might contain the protein from another food that commonly causes allergic reactions. For instance, if a peanut gene were added to another food, people with allergies to peanuts would need this information to avoid the food. These policies adequately protect and inform consumers. "There is no scientifically valued distinction between

FROM THE BENCH

Alliance for Bio-Integrity, et al. v. Shalala, (No. 98–1300 D.D.C.) 2000

In May 1998, a coalition of citizens, scientists, religious leaders, health professionals, organized by the Alliance for Bio-Integrity, filed a lawsuit in federal court against the U.S. Food and Drug Administration. The suit alleged that FDA policies regarding safety testing and labeling of genetically engineered food violate consumer rights and religious freedom, since the lack of labeling prevents people from being able to choose foods that comply with their religious beliefs.

On September 29, 2000, U.S. District Judge Colleen Kollar-Kotelly dismissed the case, saying that the plaintiffs had failed to prove that the FDA violated procedural and environmental laws in establishing its policy. The judge further stated that the agency has no duty to require labeling of GM foods. Quoting from FDA regulations, Judge Kollar-Kotelly said that the FDA policy "was not arbitrary and capricious in its finding that genetically modified foods need not be labeled because they do not differ 'materially' from nonmodified foods." The court also rejected the plaintiffs' claim that the FDA policy violated their First Amendment rights to free exercise of religion on the grounds that the policy is neutral and generally applicable to all people, regardless of religion.

the safety of genetically enhanced food and food grown by traditional methods," said Stephen Giller, vice president of the Grocery Manufacturers of America. "It would be enormously impractical to label every genetically modified new crop and would falsely imply a difference in the foods' safety."[153]

Genetic engineering can promote a cleaner environment by helping crops resist pests on their own.

Genetic engineering can actually help the environment by producing plants that need fewer pesticides and chemicals to flourish. Scientists can develop these pest-resistant plants by introducing to them genes from bacteria that produce insect toxins. A major source for this kind of gene is the *Bacillus thuringiensis* (Bt). It has been injected into the cells of corn, squash, and other plants.

Scientists have also produced plants that resist the deadly effects of herbicides, such as glyphosate, a chemical that is found in the Monsanto product called Roundup. A gene that confers this kind of resistance has been placed in corn, soybean, and canola crops. As a result, farmers can spray fields with weed-killing herbicides without harming food crops. At an international meeting of the British Crop Protection Council, Dennis Avery, director of global food issues at the Hudson Institute, said that Bt corn and so-called Roundup Ready soybeans were "wonderful examples of high-yield technologies which use some of the safest and most sustainable technologies ever used by science."[154]

People who criticize herbicide use often ignore the trade-offs involved in food production. They fail to note that some herbicides pose fewer safety hazards than others, and that alternatives are often ineffective and/or undesirable. One alternative to using herbicides is to cultivate more land, but that can cause more soil erosion and other environmental problems. Critics also say that herbicide resistance can spread from crops to weeds, making weeds harder to control. This is unlikely, since few crops are interbred with weeds (canola being an exception). Moreover, the crops would be resistant to only one kind of herbicide. If a particular plant appeared in the wild that was resistant to one herbicide, farmers could use another type.

In deciding these matters, scientists and other involved parties must make informed, case-by-case evaluations based on the costs and benefits. Spraying pesticides to protect crops from insect pests creates residues that spread through the air, affecting wildlife. For instance, during the late 1990s, American scientists said that pollen from GM corn with Bt might harm monarch butterflies. In this case, however, it was deemed that the Bt corn did not pose a serious threat to the butterflies, and so it was allowed to stay on the market. In cases where experts think a certain GM plant *would* cause serious harm to consumers or the environment, it can be kept off the market.

Genetic engineering can help ease world hunger by improving crop yields, boosting nutritional content, and producing plants that grow under poor conditions.

The world population is expected to reach about 9 billion by 2045, which will increase food needs, especially in developing nations. "The combination of more people and rising incomes will increase the demand for food by at least 50 percent in the next 25 years," said Dr. Robert B. Horsch, recipient of the 1998 National Medal of Technology for his genetic experiments with plant cells.[155]

Genetic engineering can enhance the global food supply by extending the shelf life of crops and making plants more resistant to diseases and pests. Growing GM foods also can increase profits, which encourages the food industry to produce larger quantities for the markets. The tomato market, for example, was worth about $4 billion each year during the early 1990s when the first GM tomatoes were launched.[156] Such gains can spur large agricultural companies to produce more food, and GM techniques will help this food travel across longer distances.

Diseases and pests can destroy large areas of crops and devastate the food supply of a subsistence farmer. Pest control can reduce crop losses, and some GM techniques help plants to resist destructive insects. The development of stronger, pest-resistant plants offers hope for relieving malnutrition and hunger.

Genetic engineering has conquered some plant diseases as well, and offers opportunities for the future. One solution involves a method called antisense. Normally, genes only work correctly when they face in a specific direction along the line of genes that make up a strand of DNA. When scientists insert genes in the wrong direction, they interrupt the normal activity of that gene. This method can be used to kill harmful plant viruses so they do not grow or multiply. A virus-resistant squash has been developed using antisense.

Papayas offer another good example of how genetic engineering can save a plant that is threatened by disease. In the mid 1990s, Hawaiian farmers feared that an insect-borne virus, the papaya ring spot virus (PRSV), would destroy their state's second-largest fruit crop. Traditional plant breeders were unable to produce a virus-resistant papaya. Dr. Dennis Gonsalves, a plant pathologist, led a team at Cornell University in engineering a papaya that could resist PRSV; they did this by integrating a virus gene into the chromosomes of the fruit. Starting in 1998, farmers could plant seeds of PRSV-resistant papaya, thus saving their businesses in growing this popular and nutritious fruit—"a really satisfying story," as Dr. Gonsalves concluded.[157]

New transgenic plants can survive better in poor soil or in very dry or very moist climates. Using GM plants, farmers will be able to grow larger quantities of healthy crops on smaller areas of land. The United Nations estimates that about 18,000 children die of hunger each year, noted Brian Larkins, associate vice chancellor for research at the University of Nebraska-Lincoln.[158]

"We need novel ways of producing food that we have never used before," said Larkins, who has personally spent decades studying ways to increase the protein value of corn. Through genetic engineering, the corn kernel produced twice the amount of lycin, a necessary protein for the human diet. Research continues to refine ways in which the lycin-enhanced corn plant can be produced abundantly, which will help developing nations solve nutrition problems.[159]

Plant pathologist Florence Wambugu, a native of Kenya, has predicted that GM technology can reduce food shortages and provide adequate food for some one million people, without adding to production costs. In 1992, she began working with the Monsanto Company to develop a sweet potato that can resist a viral infection that destroys large amounts of this crop, a staple in many parts of Africa. At a conference held in 2001, Wambugu called biotechnology "a powerful new tool that can help address some of the agricultural problems that plague Africa." She continued, "The protesters have fanned the flames of mistrust of genetically modified foods through a campaign of misinformation. . . . I know of what I speak because I grew up barefoot and hungry."[160]

Critics say that legal issues, especially those involving patents, will prevent GM foods from reaching people who need them. In the case of golden rice, however, the AstraZeneca company agreed the rice could be given to farmers in developing countries who earned less than $10,000 a year. The company retained the right to market rice in developed nations, such as the United States. Other companies waived their rights to the rice. "Scientists, as a privileged group of citizens, have more than an academic responsibility to advance science," said Dr. Ingo Potrykus, who helped to develop golden rice. "They must also accept a higher social responsibility and, wherever possible, use science to help solve the important problems not of industry, but of humanity."[161] Potrykus points out many ways in which golden rice exemplifies the process of using GM foods to help humankind, since it "fulfills an urgent need ... presents a sustainable, cost-free solution, not requiring other resources ... benefit[s] the poor and disadvantaged ... is given free of charge and restrictions to subsistence farmers ... can be resown every year from the saved harvest. ... does not reduce agricultural biodiversity. ..." Furthermore, Potrykus says, "There is, so far, no conceptual negative effect on the environment. There is, so far, no conceivable risk to consumer health."[162]

Summary

Although it makes sense to question some aspects of genetic engineering and require adequate testing, rejecting all GM techniques and foods is shortsighted and unreasonable. Opponents have used blanket generalizations, scare tactics, and negative names like "Frankenfood" to rouse negative emotions and taint all GM foods. GM foods are here to stay, so people need to look at them case-by-case, based on facts and taking into account the costs and benefits of using genetic engineering techniques.

Some opponents have suggested a complete moratorium on GM food production until testing conclusively proves it is safe. Such tests would take many years, however, and the results might still not completely satisfy critics. Even if scientists could show that the probability of harmful effects is extremely low, they cannot prove conclusively that there will never be any long-term ill effects, because science cannot prove a negative hypothesis. Meanwhile, people would miss out on the benefits GM foods offer, especially in developing nations where people struggle with poor soil, drought, and widespread malnutrition.

Consumers must educate themselves about GM foods so they can base their opinions and food choices on scientific facts, not unreasonable fears. Says plant researcher Dr. Robert B. Horsch, "Biotechnology is a great tool that will allow us to produce more food on less land and with less depletion or damage to water resources and biodiversity."[163]

The Regulatory Process Does Not Protect Consumers from the Hazards of Meat and Poultry Production

O n April 16, 1996, the *Oprah Winfrey Show* broadcast an episode titled "Dangerous Foods." It addressed topics relating to meat safety, including BSE—bovine spongiform encephalopathy, commonly called mad cow disease. The disease made news in the 1980s when the British government announced that BSE had passed from animals to humans as variant Creutzfeldt-Jacob disease, part of a group of diseases called TSEs (transmissible spongiform encephalopathies). Cooking does not get rid of the mutant proteins, called prions, that cause TSEs. Since the 1980s, meat products contaminated with this rare and fatal brain disease have been blamed for 150 deaths around the world.[164] Scientists said the disease arose because cows were being fed products that contained infected material from the brains and other organs of dead sheep and cattle. Britain banned this practice in 1988, and consumer groups and scientists in the United States also opposed it.

A guest on Winfrey's show, author and activist Howard Lyman, a former rancher turned vegetarian, discussed beef production in the United States. Lyman said that federal agencies should ban the use of dead animal parts in cattle feed, commenting, "We should have them eating grass, not other cows. We've not only turned them into carnivores, we've turned them into cannibals."[165] Two other guests—Dr. Gary Weber, a representative from the National Cattlemen's Beef Association, and Dr. William Hueston from the U.S. Department of Agriculture—reassured viewers that U.S. beef is safe and said the meat supply is carefully regulated.

In June 1997, the USFDA did finally ban the use of certain dead animal parts in cattle feed, but critics say billions of pounds of dead cattle material went into feed before this ban took effect.[166] In March 2006, the U.S. Department of Agriculture announced that it was investigating a possible case of BSE. Luckily, this cow had not entered the human or animal food chain, according to USDA chief veterinarian Dr. John Clifford.[167] Two other cases of this disease had turned up in 2003 and in 2005. These incidents refueled debates over policies and practices affecting meat safety. Critics say that more must be done, especially since the United States imports meat and dairy products from other countries. Government agencies cannot adequately regulate and inspect all of those items.

Bacterial contamination concerns even more people. Foodborne illnesses attributed to meat and dairy products increased after the 1970s, and most food-related deaths involve animal products. According to author Steve Striffler, "Contaminated chicken kills at least one thousand people and sickens millions of others every year in the United States."[168] One study showed that 30 percent of raw chicken was contaminated with salmonella and 62 percent with campylobacter.[169] The USDA says that these two pathogens cause 82 percent of the illnesses and 75 percent of the deaths linked to meat consumption.[170] Cross-contamination occurs unless people handle chicken carefully, and it must be cooked long enough to kill these pathogens. *Time* magazine called raw chicken "one of the most dangerous items in the American home."[171]

Food-borne pathogens can affect vast quantities of food and thousands of people. Pregnant women, the elderly, and people with impaired immune systems are most vulnerable. In 1994, an estimated 224,000 people throughout the nation contracted *Salmonella enteritidis* after eating ice cream that was shipped from one processing facility in Minnesota.[172] In 2001, about 100 million pounds of meat were involved in 163 recalls. The following

FROM THE BENCH

Texas Beef Group v. Oprah Winfrey, Harpo Productions Inc. and Howard Lyman, 11 Supp.2d 858 (N.D., 1998)

After *The Oprah Winfrey Show* aired its episode "Dangerous Foods," a group of cattlemen filed a lawsuit against Winfrey, her production company, and Howard Lyman, saying that they violated a Texas law called the False Disparagement of Perishable Food Products Act. The plaintiffs said that the comments made on the show seriously harmed the beef industry and did not adequately present opposing viewpoints. They also charged the defendants with defamation and negligence.

The case was moved to a federal court, where the judge dismissed most of the claims. A jury in Texas heard the case for business disparagement and ruled in favor of the defendants. When the cattlemen appealed, the appellate court upheld the verdict, saying, "The critical issue here is whether the appellees knowingly disseminated false information tending to show that American beef is not fit for public consumption" and concluded that "the expression of opinions as well as facts is constitutionally protected so long as a factual basis underlies the opinion."

year a large meat products company recalled 19 million pounds of beef because of potential contamination with *E. coli* 0157:H7. That summer, an outbreak of *Listeria monocytogenes*, blamed on tainted luncheon meats, left 120 people ill and 20 dead in 22 states. Cases of the listeria bacterium in processed meats and cheese have risen in recent decades. This bacterium has a long incubation period, so extensive damage can occur before the problem is identified.[173]

At one time, food production was more localized and people tended to rely on regional sources for foods. Cows and cattle grazed on the range or in pastures, and most livestock lived on family-run farms or ranches. Today's food production is more centralized and larger in scale. Food animals live in big feedlots run by multinational corporations that emphasize speed, volume, and economy. Four giant companies—Tyson/IBP, Swift and Co./ConAgra, Cargill/Excel, and Farmland National Beef—control more than 80 percent of the beef market and about 40 percent of the poultry market.

Many experts blame current methods of raising, feeding, and processing livestock and meat products for the increase in bacterial contamination. Infections can spread in places where animals are raised and in processing plants. In the 2002 PBS special *Modern Meat*, Dr. Robert Tauxe, head of the food-borne illness division of the Centers for Disease Control (CDC), said, "Industrialization of our meat supply opened up a conduit for salmonella, for campylobacter, for *E. coli* 0157:H7 infections."[174]

In addition to food poisoning, these infections may cause other health problems. According to Christopher Cook, "A host of chronic ailments, including reactive arthritis, Reiter's syndrome, Miller-Fisher syndrome, and ulcers, have now been linked to bacterial infections often caused by contaminated foods."[175] Scientists have been exploring a link between *Campylobacter jejuni* bacteria and a serious autoimmune condition called Guillain-Barre syndrome (GBS), which can lead to neuromuscular paralysis.[176] GBS afflicts between 500 and nearly 4,000 Americans each year.[177]

Other hazards arise from methods used to fatten and process animals. Hormone implants are used to make cattle grow faster and larger. Animals are given foods that are unnatural for their digestive system and their feed frequently contains pesticide residues. Critics also fault methods used to process animals and say regulatory and inspection systems should do more to ensure safe meat and poultry.

Factory farming allows diseases to spread more easily, leading to the routine use of antibiotics.

Pathogens can spread quickly among animals in the conditions that typify the meat production industry. Cattle from diverse places are brought together in barns that may lack adequate sanitation facilities. Large numbers of animals live in tight quarters and even spend all their time in one space, standing and sleeping amid their waste products. Some buildings house 50,000 to 100,000 chickens, and a turkey may have just three feet of living space.

About 9 billion chickens are raised annually in the United States, usually in factory farms, and statistics show widespread contamination in poultry and eggs. Most factory-farmed hens do not hatch eggs themselves; instead, eggs are hatched in sterile incubators and the chicks do not move about outdoors as they once did. Natural hatching and movement outdoors helps baby chicks to gain a natural immunity to salmonella and other organisms as they ingest droppings containing bacteria. When the Consumers Union tested whole broiler chickens in 2006, they found that 83 percent were contaminated with salmonella and/or campylobacter, an increase over the rate of 49 percent they found in 2003.[178]

Most of the cattle, swine, dairy cows, and poultry in the United States receive antibiotics to prevent diseases. These antibiotics are usually added to their feed. The first antibiotics came

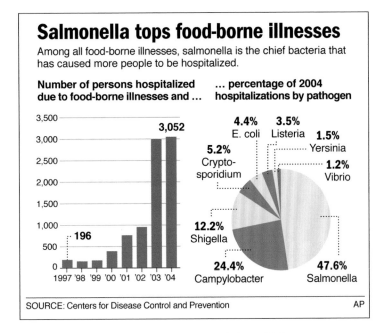

Salmonella tops food-borne illnesses

Among all food-borne illnesses, salmonella is the chief bacteria that has caused more people to be hospitalized.

Number of persons hospitalized due to food-borne illnesses and ...

... percentage of 2004 hospitalizations by pathogen

3,052

196

1997 '98 '99 '00 '01 '02 '03 '04

4.4% E. coli   **3.5%** Listeria   **1.5%** Yersinia

5.2% Crypto-sporidium

1.2% Vibrio

12.2% Shigella

24.4% Campylobacter

47.6% Salmonella

SOURCE: Centers for Disease Control and Prevention   AP

Salmonella is a bacterium that can infect chickens, eggs, dairy products, and beef. In 2004, salmonella was the cause of more hospitalizations than any other food-borne illnesses, as shown in the graphic above.

into use in 1927 after British biologist Alexander Fleming accidentally discovered the substance known as penicillin. According to author Christopher Cook, during the mid 1980s, about 16 million pounds of antibiotics were used for animal feed, a figure that reached 25 million pounds by 2001.[179] The Union of Concerned Scientists has said that about 70 percent of all the antibiotics and related drugs produced in the United States go to poultry and livestock.[180]

During the late 1940s, farmers noticed that when chicks were fed antibiotics to resist disease, they gained about 10 to 20 percent more weight than chicks on a normal diet. Cows also grow faster and require less food when low-dose antibiotics are added to their diet. This gave food producers yet another reason to give antibiotics to their livestock.

Problems can arise, however, especially if antibiotics are misused. And residues remain in animal flesh after they are slaughtered, which means that consumers also ingest these antibiotics. Some residues cannot be detected with routine testing. Resistant bacteria are another problem, especially when bacteria become resistant to more than one antibiotic. They can pass on this resistance to other bacteria and even to people. The World Health Organization (WHO) has called antibiotic resistance one of the three top threats to public health. When people are infected with a resistant organism, doctors may have to try several drugs to find one that works, if any of them work at all. A 2001 article in the *New England Journal of Medicine* stated that up to 80 percent of the chicken, pork, and beef sampled from supermarkets contained various antibiotic-resistant bacteria, and those germs could survive for a week or two in people's intestines after they ate the meat. Tests done by the Consumers Union in 2006 showed that 84 percent of the salmonella organisms and 67 percent of the campylobacter in chickens were resistant to one or more antibiotics.[181] Since 1995, the chickens have received fluoroquinolones to treat campylobacter, now the leading cause of food-borne illness in the United States. They became resistant and that resistance became more widespread after the 1990s.

Animals receive other drugs, too, including medicines to kill parasites. Substances to inhibit mold also are added to animal feed. According to the Center for Science in the Public Interest (CSPI), some of these drugs have caused cancer in laboratory animals.[182] Problems may also occur when meat producers ignore regulations that set a specific waiting period between the time an animal receives drugs and the slaughtering date. As a result, the levels of these substances in the animal's flesh exceed permissible limits.

Hormones used to fatten animals are unhealthy for consumers.

People also express concerns about hormone residues in beef. After researchers found that hormones could increase growth rates in cattle and poultry, a synthetic form of estrogen called DES came into use during the 1950s. Cattle that received DES gained 15 to 19 percent more weight than cattle that did not receive DES. This hormone was banned in 1979 after scientists found that it increased the risk of vaginal cancer in women whose mothers had received it during pregnancy to help prevent miscarriages. New kinds of growth hormones were then developed for use in livestock.

The U.S. government now bans hormone use in pork and poultry but permits its use in cattle. Pellets containing growth hormone are typically implanted in the steers' ears when they reach the feedlot, at ages six to eight months. From their birth weight of about 80 pounds (about 36 kilograms), cattle reach their slaughtering weight of about 1,200 pounds (about 550 kilograms) in as little as 14 months—much sooner than the three years this process required in the 1950s.[183]

Hormones can remain in animal tissues after slaughtering, and this "pervasive use of hormones in animals presents public health risks," according to the CSPI. "Some of these risks are associated with illegal residues resulting from the misuse of the drugs, which government inspections usually don't catch. But residues in concentrations below the legal limits may also present risks."[184] Risks include abnormally early puberty in children who eat foods containing hormones, ovarian cysts, and cancer of the uterus.[185]

Inspections have turned up cases of illegal hormones. In early 2004, USDA inspectors found that veal calves in two slaughterhouses had received synthetic testosterone implants— a practice banned by FDA regulations. The USDA kept these calves out of the meat supply until the drug left their systems, but they were then allowed to be sold for meat. Critics note that it is impossible to know the extent of illegal use, because lab tests are not run on most animal carcasses.[186]

An unnatural diet, including animal byproducts, increases risks for consumers.

Producers look for economical sources of food, including protein sources, and the use of growth hormones increases an animal's food needs. Although the government banned cattle brain and spinal tissue from cattle feed, other animal byproducts are still used to feed cattle, as well as poultry and hogs. Along with corn and soybean meal, hogs and chickens receive ground-up bone and meat byproducts from various animals. Cattle feed may legally contain poultry manure, blood and blood products, grease, and pork and horsemeat byproducts.[187]

Cows, sheep, and goats (as well as a few other animals) are known as ruminants. A ruminant's digestive system is specially designed to break down grass and other coarse plant materials. Although cattle are natural grass eaters, feedlot cattle receive a concentrated and starchy diet that can cause digestive disorders, with bloating, excess acid, ulcers, diarrhea, and other health problems. "Cattle sent to industrial-style feedlots in their final weeks before slaughter ... are fed a diet consisting primarily of corn and other grains," said the Union of Concerned Scientists. "This unnatural diet ... can cause diseases such as liver abscesses. These diseases are one reason that feedlot owners lace feed with antibiotics—to treat illnesses created by their choice of feed and management techniques."[188]

Such feeding practices also affect the environment. The National Corn Growers Association has said that about 80 percent of the corn grown in the United States goes for livestock feed worldwide. To produce large crops, corn growers often use more pesticides and other chemicals. Animal feed may therefore contain pesticides, even illegal kinds. In 1978, for example, heptachlor was banned for use on food products, but people were allowed to use up stocks of grain treated with heptachlor so long as they kept this grain out of the food chain. Nonetheless, tainted feed was purposely or accidentally mixed with other seeds and fed to animals. During the 1980s, residues of heptachlor turned up in thousands of chickens.

Conditions at processing plants can cause food safety problems.

The methods used to kill and process animals often make contamination more likely. Problems can arise when plant workers are required to handle meat and poultry at high rates of speed. In *Diet for a Dead Planet*, Christopher Cook notes that poultry lobbyists succeeded in raising the permissible processing line speeds during the 1980s from 70 birds per minute to 90. As a result, says Cook, "ninety chicken parts speed by workers and inspectors every sixty seconds."[189] The meatpacking industry also increased the number of pieces per minute on its lines. During the 1970s, workers in that industry butchered about 175 cattle per hour; by 2002, that rate had more than doubled.[190]

Profit margins are not high in this industry, so fast production can lower costs. Although such practices benefit producers and keep prices lower for consumers, they increase the chance of bacterial contamination. According to one critic, "... research has shown that most bacterial contamination is the result of spillage onto meat of eviscerated stomach contents, hide removal, and worker-to-meat transferred bacteria. The faster the production, the greater the chance of contamination."[191] When people work too fast, they may drop meat and put it back on the line, spill manure on carcasses, and improperly gut the meat.

Fast-moving line speeds can cause other problems: They make it more difficult for USDA inspectors to spot signs of contamination on the line. Workers can suffer strain injuries, accidents, and even permanent disabilities. A report issued in 2005 by Government Accountability Office (GAO) concluded that the nation's meat and poultry processing plants had "one of the highest rates of injury and illness of any industry" and that workers were exposed to "dangerous chemicals, blood, fecal matter, exacerbated by poor ventilation and often extreme temperatures."[192] Many workers also cope with loud noises while working in small spaces with sharp tools and dangerous machinery. In 2005, Human Rights Watch reported, "Nearly every worker interviewed for this report bore serious signs of a physical injury suffered from working in a meat or poultry plant. Automated lines carrying dead animals and their parts for disassembly move too fast for worker safety."[193]

Other processing practices arouse criticism, too. Poultry carcasses have typically been rinsed all together in the same water, something critics call a communal bath. This process can spread microorganisms to all of the poultry that touch this

FROM THE BENCH

APHA v. Butz, 511 F. 2nd (1974)

In this case, the American Public Health Association (APHA) sued then-Secretary of Agriculture Earl Butz. In light of the frequent presence of salmonella and other bacteria, APHA said the USDA could not assure consumers that meat products were safe and that its stamp of approval was therefore misleading. They asked the department to require warning labels on meat and poultry alerting consumers to the presence of pathogens.

The court ruled in favor of the defendant, saying that such labels were unnecessary. The judges wrote, "American housewives and cooks normally are not ignorant or stupid and their methods of preparing and cooking of food do not ordinarily result in salmonellosis." The court also said that bacteria were inherent to meats and that the USDA seal of approval was not intended to promise that all products were free from bacteria.

Decades passed before the government changed its decision about such labels, leading to the safe handling instructions found on meat and poultry products today.

water. And to make ground beef, the meat from hundreds and even thousands of different cows is added to machines that grind meat by the ton. This means that bacteria from any animal can reach the whole batch.

Inspection procedures and regulations do not guarantee safe products.

Critics charge that government agencies do not have enough inspectors to effectively monitor meat, poultry, and dairy products. As a result, inspections are neither as thorough nor as frequent as they need to be. The meat industry is also criticized for exerting too much control and influence over government policy.

The area of meat regulation again shows how the functions of different agencies can overlap. In the FDA, the Center for Veterinary Medicine oversees animal food and the Center for Food Safety and Applied Nutrition oversees humans' food products and additives. The USDA also has authority—over safety issues involving meat, poultry, and eggs sold through interstate commerce, except for game meats, which come under the FDA. The Food Safety and Inspection Service (FSIS) of the USDA inspects meat and poultry products and regulates food and color additives used in them. Its Agricultural Marketing Service (AMS) inspects eggs and egg products. The FDA regulates drugs given to animals, while the USDA regulates the biologic drugs (given to prevent disease or illness) they receive. A company that processes both vegetable and meat products can fall under the jurisdiction of the FDA, the USDA, and the state in which it operates. As a result, problems may require intervention by more than one agency. When the case of mad cow disease was discovered in December 2003, for example, USDA officials searched for all the beef that was processed from the carcass while the FDA analyzed what that cow had eaten.

Special interest groups, including meat and poultry associations, often fight government proposals designed to label their products or inspect products more closely. Despite outbreaks of listeria, food companies protested the idea of mandatory microbial testing in ready-to-eat foods.[194] Over strong objections by the food industry, the USDA did finally list *E. coli* as a food adulterant in 1994, a standard that would make a company legally liable for selling meat contaminated with these bacteria. When the USDA proposed testing for *E. coli,* the American Meat Institute joined other industry groups in filing a lawsuit to halt the plan. Opponents said this rule was unfair because salmonella in poultry was not likewise treated as an adulterant. As of 2006, the USDA required chicken producers to check for salmonella but not campylobacter, even though the latter has become more common.

For years, the meat industry fought proposals to put safe handling labels on their products. Sometimes the USDA seemed to agree with them. In 1993, then-USDA chief Mike Espy was asked about using labels that would warn consumers about possible pathogens in poultry products. He replied, "We wouldn't do anything like that. We don't want to have a chilling effect on sales."[195]

At times, the USDA did recommend safe handling labels, but it failed to act until after several children died in January 1993 from eating restaurant hamburgers infected with *E. coli* O157:H7. An organization called Beyond Beef, which included parents of the victims, sued the USDA to require instructions for consumers on meat and poultry packages. The court ruled in their favor and directed the USDA to "mandate labels regarding the handling and cooking of meat and poultry to minimize the chance that bacterial contamination will reach the consumer."[196] Still, members of the meat industry continued to say these labels might frighten consumers by implying that products were unsafe. They managed to delay the required labeling, which did take effect late in 1993.

As for the inspection process, CSPI noted that inspectors spend about 10 seconds checking each beef carcass that passes on a conveyor belt, although carcasses can weigh 1,000 pounds (about 450 kilograms). Poultry inspectors examine some 90 birds per minute.[197] Inspectors view and smell the meat for signs of spoilage but do not typically use a microscope or lab testing that can detect microorganisms.

To complicate matters, food comes from many sources and travels far and fast. "The meat in a typical fast-food hamburger could contain bits of beef from a hundred different cows from a dozen states and several foreign countries," notes CSPI. "A single contaminated cow could infect thousands of burgers from Maine to Hawaii."[198] Meat might be frozen and kept for months before it is used, so some people consume it long before other people do. This makes it difficult for inspectors to see connections among illnesses or to determine where the infected product originated.

To improve safety, the USDA implemented HACCP (Hazard Analysis and Critical Control Point), a system that evolved from a food safety program designed for the National Aeronautics and Space Administration (NASA). NASA needed to verify that any foods astronauts consumed during space missions would be safe. In 1971, it instituted HACCP in order to control the production process, raw materials, environment, and employees working with the foods. HACCP requires food producers to examine every phase of their work to spot potential hazards and identify critical control points where contamination can occur. Then they must design a plan to prevent contamination during each step of production.

Critics say that even if HACCP is an improvement, the system does not go far enough and is not always used properly. Line speeds at processing plants remain rapid. The companies themselves have much control over the process, since they choose the number and location of critical control points. "Factory farms do their own testing of meats under USDA supervision," said a former meat inspector in 1998. "It's like the wolf guarding the henhouse."[199] Inspectors have said they were told to be careful in making any decisions that could slow down or stop the line, because the company could sue them.[200] Some USDA inspectors also consider this new system weaker than previous inspection methods. After observing and interviewing people working in a meat processing plant with a HACCP system, author Marion Nestle wrote, "... it seemed obvious that HACCP plans can prevent contamination but that diligence in following them is not enough; the plans also must be thoughtfully designed and overseen, and verified by testing."[201]

HACCP provides yet another example of how change comes slowly in the area of food safety. People advocated such changes for 20 years before HACCP was implemented in 1996. Concerns about antibiotic resistance have also been ignored. After years of pressure from consumer groups, the FDA did finally withdraw its approval of fluoroquinolone for use in poultry and recommended using Enrofloxacin instead. In their defense, government agencies cite intense pressure from the food industry. When the FDA considered banning the non-therapeutic use of antibiotics in animals, the drug and livestock industries lobbied Congress to prevent the FDA from taking this step.

In April 2007, Senator Tom Harkin, a Democrat from Iowa, called for an audit of the nation's food safety system. He wrote:

> From human food-borne illnesses linked to spinach, toma-toes, and peanut butter, to kidney failure in companion animals caused by the chemical melamine in pet food, the breakdowns in our nation's food and feed safety system are impacting consumers and producers alike. We must have a comprehensive assessment of the food safety system to learn how we can better protect the United States food supply.[202]

Summary

Today's methods of factory farming produce food that is more likely to contain pathogens and antibiotic and hormone residues, besides harming animals and the environment. Instead of using drugs to promote growth and treat diseases, food producers should improve the living conditions of the animals. Giving animals adequate space, ventilation, natural light, and cleaner surroundings offers real hope of reducing diseases that can taint meat and poultry products. Livestock can be raised without hormones, antibiotics, and other chemical feed additives. At the very least, food producers can use antibiotics that are not used in treating human illnesses. Reducing the line speeds and making sure that workers have proper training, equipment, and working conditions also can enhance quality control at processing plants.

Growth hormone implants were banned in Europe during the 1990s, along with certain antibiotics, yet the United States has not done likewise. Agricultural economist Charles Benbrook notes, "The U.S. is likely to slip farther behind food safety leaders internationally as long as our leaders and public institutions remain in denial that the way we raise, manufacture, distribute, and cook food has opened the door to some significant new risks."[203]

Modern Production Methods and Regulatory Procedures Provide Consumers With Quality Meats

P eople took notice in 2006 when the U.S. Department of Agriculture (USDA) said it was investigating a possible case of BSE (bovine spongiform encephalopathy), commonly called mad cow disease. This announcement brought renewed complaints against the meat industry and the government agencies that oversee meat production. The test results that spurred the investigation showed up during routine tests done on cattle to prevent BSE from entering the food chain. As USDA chief veterinarian Dr. John Clifford said, "Inconclusive results are a normal part of most screening tests, which are designed to be extremely sensitive."[204] The USDA expanded its BSE testing in 2003 after finding a case of the disease in a Canadian-born cow that was raised in the United States. These sophisticated tests are used on cows that have died or on live cows that cannot walk, are injured, or show signs of a nervous system disorder or other illness. As of 2006, three tests had yielded "inconclusive" results.

Further testing showed that none of the three cows was infected with BSE.

These testing procedures are among numerous safeguards that protect people from BSE. Since 1986, U.S. government agencies have instigated 33 policies and control measures designed to prevent an infected cow from reaching the food supply. Since 1989, the USDA has banned the importation of ruminant animals (cattle, sheep, and goats) and their by-products from the United Kingdom, where people have died from BSE. That ban was extended to all European countries. It is also illegal to add parts from dead cattle to feed designated for live cattle, since this may spread BSE from animal to animal. And when slaughtering animals, processing plants must remove tissues known to carry BSE, including the brain and spinal cord. As of 2004, new regulations banned "downer cows"—cows that cannot walk—from being fed to humans after slaughter. In 2005, the FDA proposed more safeguards, banning the use of any high-risk cattle materials in the feed of any animal.

These measures reassure people, including scientific experts. Dr. John Clifford has said, "We remain very confident in the safety of U.S. beef."[205] Paul Brown, an epidemiologist at the National Institute of Neurological Disorders and Stroke who also chairs a panel that advises the FDA on mad cow disease, expressed a similar opinion. "Beef produced in the U.S. is free from BSE, so consumers shouldn't worry," Brown said.[206]

Bacterial illnesses from meat products arouse other concerns, but reports from the Centers for Disease Control (CDC) show that these diseases are declining. In March 2000, a report from the Foodborne Diseases Active Surveillance Network showed that illnesses from the most common food-borne pathogens declined almost 20 percent between 1997 and 1999. This meant that 855,000 fewer Americans were contracting such illnesses than in previous years. Noting these statistics, then-Secretary of Agriculture Dan Glickman said, "The reported declines in food-borne disease, particularly in campylobacter and *E. coli* O157: H7, are encouraging and suggest that our prevention efforts are paying off."[207] In 2004, a joint report from the CDC, FDA, and USDA showed that the rates of infections from food-borne pathogens declined even further than they had between 1996 and 1998.

Other studies show lower rates of bacterial contamination in meat and poultry than critics have claimed. In 2006, the Consumers Union found a contamination rate of 81 percent when they tested chickens, but a larger study conducted by the USDA found rates of campylobacter were about 26 percent.[208] Bacterial contamination of ground beef has decreased significantly, and positive tests for *E. coli* dropped by about 80 percent (to 0.17 percent) between 2000 and 2006.

With its livelihood at stake, the industry itself has addressed bacterial contamination and other problems in meat and poultry products. Producers and sellers use scientific, technological, and educational tools to make foods as safe as possible and maximize production in ways that enable them to deliver meat and poultry at affordable prices.

Factory-style production is efficient and profitable, which benefits consumers and society.

Meat and poultry products remain a major source of dietary protein for people in many parts of the world. Americans consume relatively large quantities of these foods. They are regarded as a sign of prosperity, as reflected in a political adage from the 1920s: "A chicken in every pot." A rapidly expanding world population means even greater demand, so meat companies aim to maximize production, including raising large numbers of animals together as efficiently and inexpensively as possible. They have found ways to raise more animals on smaller areas of land where they can be fed and tended to faster and more easily.

Although critics oppose so-called "factory" farms and feedlots, large companies can offer advantages for consumers. Former Secretary of Agriculture Dan Glickman points out, "Mass industrialization and standardization probably can ensure quality control better because somebody's watching the product at all stages of the scheme."[209] Large companies usually can afford more equipment, including products that improve testing and sanitation—for example, machines that wash and even steam-clean meat carcasses.

Profit margins are small in this industry and consolidation can help businesses to survive and keep prices down. Supporters of large-scale meat production methods note that in 2002, consumers were paying about 30 percent less for meat than they did in 1970. "Americans pay a lower per capita cost for food of all types than any place else in the world," Glickman said.[210]

Although critics complain that large-scale production leads to more bacterial contamination, this problem also occurs in livestock raised by smaller companies, including brands labeled "organic." In December 2006, the Consumers Union reported on a study it conducted in 23 states with chickens from supermarkets, mass retailers, gourmet shops, and natural food stores. They found bacteria in leading brands, lesser known brands, and organic chickens alike.[211] Some studies find higher rates of contamination in organic chickens and free-range chickens than in conventionally raised birds. These animals might make more contact with the feces of other animals, including wild birds, than chickens raised in cages. Ctitics also cite inadequate standards and enforcement in the organic food industry.

Members of the beef industry have found practical and effective ways to reduce contamination in cattle. These include supplements that contain beneficial bacteria in the form of lactobacilli. These organisms help to lower the pH level in the intestines, which discourages the growth of *E. coli* 0157. Scientists are also working on vaccines that prevent that bacterium, and they are testing their live animals and products more often to identify and control contamination sooner.

The use of licensed antibiotics enhances food safety and poses no proven dangers.

Antibiotics offer producers an important tool for keeping livestock healthier and reducing the spread of disease, thus protecting consumers. Salmonella and other bacteria are the leading cause of food-borne illnesses, so it makes sense to prevent and control these infections in animals. Antibiotics also kill parasites that animals can acquire while grazing on forage infested with larvae. Bovine respiratory disease is the most common reason that cows require antibiotic treatment, and it occurs in similar rates among cattle in pastures and in feedlots.[212]

Laws regulate the use of antibiotics for chickens, cattle, cows, and swine. The animals receive sub-therapeutic doses— relatively low doses set at levels that can combat pathogens and enhance growth. Samples of livestock and poultry tissues are collected at slaughtering facilities and checked for residues of animal drugs.[213] A National Research Council (NRC) scientific committee concluded that the current monitoring systems used for detecting drug residues in meat and other animal food products are adequate. "There is a relatively large safety margin in the use of animal drugs when proper withdrawal times and uses are followed," the NRC committee said.[214]

Critics have said that antibiotics should only be given to food animals to treat specific diseases. The NRC committee examined the consequences of this approach and concluded that

FROM THE BENCH

Supreme Beef v. USDA, Fifth Circuit Court of Appeals (2001)

Supreme Beef Processors Inc. sued the U.S. Department of Agriculture after the USDA shut down its beef-grinding plant in Texas following the failure of three series of tests for salmonella contamination. The court ruled in favor of Supreme Beef, saying that the USDA could not shut down a meat processing plant based solely on salmonella tests. The meat industry supported this decision, saying that the presence of salmonella on raw, uncooked meat does not constitute a public health risk, in and of itself.

public health risks might increase if the rates of animal diseases increased, requiring more antibiotics to treat those sick animals. The Institute of Food Technologists (IFT) in Chicago, a non-profit international scientific society, discussed this matter in its report *Antimicrobial Resistance: Implications for the Food System.* The IFT said that in some cases, removing antibiotics from animal feed abroad did lead to more antibiotic use, as well as more resistant bacteria.

The public expresses concern about new, antibiotic-resistant forms of bacteria. The NRC report acknowledged this possibility, but noted a lack of data in terms of sources of illness and shifts in disease rates: "It has been difficult to track and document the link between antibiotic use in farm animals, the development of antibiotic resistance, and disease transference to humans."[215] A very low number of cases of human illnesses can be traced to antibiotic-resistant germs in food animals, the committee said. It concluded that resistant bacteria are most likely to cause illness through improper food processing, storing, or cooking procedures.

The NRC report further estimated that banning antibiotic use except for treating illnesses would raise prices for poultry, beef, and fish. This would cost consumers about $1.2 billion to $2.5 billion a year, or about $4.85 to $9.72 per person.[216]

Diets for feedlot animals are designed to meet their nutritional needs in an efficient and cost-effective manner.

Critics complain that feedlot animals are mistreated and eat an unnatural diet they would not consume in the pasture or farmyard. But feedlot operator Bill Haw points out that "... a very nutritious and very palatable diet is delivered to them upon demand."[217]

Most cattle raised for beef graze in pastures when they are about 8 to 10 months old. Then they are moved to feedlots—called concentrated animal feeding operations (CAFO). There, they eat a diet that usually contains corn and other grains, which produces meat marbleized with a certain amount of fat. Consumers consider this meat juicier, more tender, and more richly flavored than meat from grass-fed cattle. In a 2003 study, 80 percent of Americans preferred the taste of corn-fed beef over grass-fed.

Producing grass-feed beef with similar qualities requires more time and other resources. Keeping all cattle on grasslands would require more space, and there is not enough western grazing land to accommodate the 100 million cattle being raised in the United States. Grass-fed cattle are not slaughtered until they are 24 to 30 months old, compared to 14 to 18 months for cattle on CAFO diets. Grass-fed cattle are slaughtered mainly in the autumn, since grass lies dormant in the wintertime. To improve flavor and texture, grass-fed beef also is aged for about three weeks.

A CAFO diet usually includes animal protein supplements. Despite claims by critics, the use of animal protein in feed is not new or inherently dangerous. The poultry industry was using fish meal, meat scraps, and dried skim milk in feed by the 1800s. They found that this diet was better for chickens than an all-plant diet and it reduced waste products from animal processing. Scientists, including nutritionists, microbiologists, toxicologists, and veterinarians, have found effective ways to render proteins for nutritious animal diets. Veterinarian Gary G. Pearl writes, "Today there are no scientific reasons that animal protein ingredients are not safe food ingredients for poultry or livestock, companion animal and aquaculture rations."[218]

Rendered animal proteins come from meat and bonemeal, meat meal, poultry meal, hydrolyzed feather meal, and blood and fish meals. Adding enzymes to these tissues breaks down the material, making it digestible.[219] Dr. Pearl says:

> The rendering process is a biosecure proven process, which
> evaporates water, extracts fat, and results in approximately

a 25 percent fat and a 25 percent protein yield from the raw material. The process completely decharacterizes muscle and other tissues into protein rich granular type substrates and fats with specific nutritional components that has absolutely no resemblance to the original raw material."[220]

Each year, the byproduct tissues from various food animals total about 50 billion pounds. In poultry production, for example, about 60 percent of the chicken is sold as meat, leaving 40 percent in the form of feathers, skin, fat, bone, and tissues. Rendering them into protein and fat recycles them into food; discarding them could create more public health risks. Using by-products in feed is also economical, and lower animal feed prices mean lower meat prices. Between 2000 and 2007, poultry producers saw rising production costs, including the cost of feed. Corn prices doubled with the increased demand for ethanol fuel, which is made from corn. Soybean prices also rose.

Feed supplements are regulated by law and within the industry itself. For example, large meat buyers, such as the McDonald's restaurant chain, have required suppliers to document that their cattle have not consumed any banned substances. In 2001, Richard Sellers, spokesman for the American Feed Industry Association, said that member plants took action to prevent accidental mixing of feed. "We're calling for the complete removal of ruminant-derived meat-and-bonemeal from those plants that make feed for cattle," Sellers said. "We've already set up an independent third-party certification program to verify that our members are following all FDA regulations about the proper labeling of their products."[221]

Using legally approved hormone implants is safe and beneficial.

For several decades, hormones have been implanted into food animals with no proven harmful effects on humans. Hormone implants cause animals to gain weight faster, which produces a more tender and flavorful product. This increases the meat supply while reducing the energy and feed costs per animal. Implants cost about one to three dollars and increase a steer's weight from 5 to 15 percent—a high return on the investment. Lower production costs also help to keep meat prices lower. According to Cornell University's Institute for Comparative and Environmental Toxicology, using growth hormones can "help reduce the waiting time and the amount of feed eaten by an animal before slaughter."[222] Rancher Tim Bare points out, "It actually increases the quality of the animal, producing a leaner, red meat. It's a more desirable carcass." He adds, "We're not going to do anything that will harm the animals we raise. Our goal is to utilize the forage we raise through our livestock and to raise the highest quality product we can."[223]

Three of the five hormones used in food animals—estradiol, progesterone, and testosterone—occur naturally in humans, other animals, and plants. The two approved synthetic hormones mimic the effects of natural hormones. "Some plant foods such as potatoes and wheat contain significant levels of progesterone, and other foods, including some oils and wheat, have measurable levels of testosterone," writes author Ellin Doyle. "In addition, many plants contain other compounds with estrogenic activity."[224] Because these hormones stay in the animal's system only a few months, they are usually gone by slaughtering time. Estradiol is found in much higher concentrations per portion in eggs and milk than in an implanted steer.

Federal agencies have determined safe levels for these hormones and use sensitive tools to measure residues in samples of meat tissues. Experts say the levels of hormone residues in consumer meat and poultry are too low to harm human health. Studies have shown similar levels of hormones in the tissues of slaughtered cattle that did receive hormones and those that did not.[225] Even when levels for one or more hormones were higher in the edible tissues of implanted cattle, these levels were below the levels the FDA allows.[226]

Dr. Gary Smith, professor of meat sciences at the Center for Red Meat Safety at Colorado State University, analyzed scientific findings regarding hormone levels. He found that a 3-ounce (85 gram) steak from a nonimplanted animal contained an average of 1.3 nanograms of estrogen, 0.3 nanograms of testosterone, and 0.3 nanograms of progesterone, compared to an average of 1.9 nanograms of estrogen, 0.6 nanograms of testosterone, and 0.5 nanograms of progesterone for a 3-ounce serving from an implanted animal. "There's no (statistical) difference," Smith said. To put these quantities in perspective, each day the average adult male produces 136,000 nanograms of estrogen, 6.4 million nanograms of testosterone, and 410,000 nanograms of progesterone.[227]

For its part, the FDA continues to permit hormone implants, saying:

> Consumers are not at risk from eating food from animals treated with these compounds. . . . Numerous scientific studies have demonstrated that, when these drugs are used in accordance with their approved conditions of use, concentrations of the hormones in edible tissues remain within the normal physiological range that has been established for untreated animals of the same age and sex.[228]

Agencies and lawmakers regulate and monitor meat and poultry products to protect consumers.

Government food safety agencies aim to ensure meat safety through a system of regulations, inspections, and consumer education. Meat and poultry receive the highest level of federal oversight and are the only products in the United States that receive an actual government stamp of approval. As they have done for more than a century, USDA inspectors monitor slaughterhouses and processing plants. They spot-check for chemical and physical problems and are present at least part of the day.

National system to track the transient life of beef cows

A typical beef cow will be sold and shipped several times before becoming dinner, the Department of Agriculture hopes to implement a national system in the next few years to trace where any cow has been and when to identify sources of disease.

A radio frequency identification tag containing a unique id number is attached to the calf's ear.

Each time the cow is sold or moved, the tag is scanned and the information sent to a central database.

If disease is discovered, the cow's history can be traced.

Birth-8 months	9-17 months	18-24 months
A calf is born in the spring and nursed by its mother before being weaned in the fall.	At a feed lot, cows gain three pounds a day from an energy rich diet of corn, soy, and hay.	On reaching full maturity the cow is sold to a packing plant, with a few days to live.
Weight: 90 lbs	600-800 pounds	1,300-1,500 pounds

SOURCES: Animal and Range Sciences Department, Montana State University; U.S. Department of Agriculture

Dan DeLorenzo • AP

Modern methods of communication have made tracking animals throughout their lives much easier. In 2004, the Department of Agriculture implemented a new national system to track a beef cow over the course of its lifetime in order to be able to trace outbreaks of disease.

In recent years, the government has focused more attention on prevention and early detection of problems. During the 1990s, the government required the meat industry to implement HACCP (Hazard Analysis and Critical Control Point) programs, an approach that systematically addresses each stage of production. The USDA called HACCP more strategic and smarter than spot-checking plants and observing products en route to market. Under HACCP, companies must keep records of the results of their monitoring systems. This shows investigators how well they are following safety laws over the long term. As this program took effect in 1996, Gary M. Weber, director of animal health and meat inspection for the National Cattlemen's Association, said, "We're very pleased that after a 10-year struggle to redesign the meat inspection program, we're at the first stages of implementing a modern, scientific-based prevention system."[229] Studies have shown declining rates of meat-borne bacterial illnesses since HACCP programs were installed in 1996. By 2002, for example, the incidence of salmonella levels in ground beef had declined by 44 percent.

In the 2002 PBS program *Modern Meat,* representatives from the Jack in the Box restaurant chain described safety measures they had adopted based on HACCP concepts. They include clean cutting surfaces, correct temperatures for storage and cooking meat, and safety clothing for all employees. At the grinding plant, beef patties are pulled every 15 minutes for microbial testing. Safety expert Dave Theno said that this approach involved "controlling from source all the way through production in their plants."[230]

Critics say that HACCP systems give the industry too much control while taking authority from the government. The government, however, still has the authority it needs to examine and close down plants. In 2002, Undersecretary of Agriculture Dr. Elsa Murano said, "We shut down plants all the time. Last year alone, we took about 200 enforcement actions in plants in the United States."[231] Mandatory recall authority for meat, poultry, and other food products might be necessary if companies did not cooperate with government agencies, but, as American Meat Institute CEO Patrick Boyle points out, "USDA, in their 100 years of regulating the meat industry, cannot point to a single instance where at their suggestion a company refused to initiate a voluntary recall."[232] This makes practical sense for the industry: The government announces its recalls, so companies could face serious financial consequences, including lawsuits, if they did not promptly recall questionable products.

Government agencies are collaborating to learn more about food-borne illnesses and track them down. The USDA, Health and Human Services (with CDC and FDA involvement), and state departments of health formed the Foodborne Diseases Active Surveillance Network (FoodNet). Health and Human Services (HHS) announced a related step for food safety using DNA technology:

In 1998, to improve detection and investigation of outbreaks, CDC launched a collaborative interagency initiative called PulseNet that uses DNA fingerprinting to characterize food-borne bacteria. Today, the more than 35 laboratories in CDC's PulseNet network can fingerprint *E. coli* O157:H7 strains in less than 24 hours, and share the results electronically with others in the network.[233]

The Seven HACCP Principles

Principle 1: *Conduct a hazard analysis.*
Plants determine the food safety hazards, identify the preventive measures the plant can apply to control these hazards.

Principle 2: *Identify critical control points.*
A critical control point (CCP) is a point, step, or procedure in a food process at which control can be applied and, as a result, a food safety hazard can be prevented, eliminated, or reduced to an acceptable level. A food safety hazard is any *biological, chemical,* or *physical* property that may cause a food to be unsafe for human consumption.

Principle 3: *Establish critical limits for each critical control point.*
A *critical limit* is the maximum or minimum value to which a physical, biological, or chemical hazard must be controlled at a critical control point to prevent, eliminate, or reduce to an acceptable level.

Principle 4: *Establish critical control point monitoring requirements.*
Monitoring activities are necessary to ensure that the process is under control at each critical control point. FSIS is requiring that each monitoring procedure and its frequency be listed in the HACCP plan.

Principle 5: *Establish corrective actions.*
These are actions to be taken when monitoring indicates a deviation from an established critical limit. The final rule requires a plant's HACCP plan to identify the corrective actions to be taken if a critical limit is not met. Corrective actions are intended to ensure that no

December 1999 brought a new federal plan to improve egg safety and decrease the incidence of *Salmonella enteritidis*. This comprehensive plan identifies public health practices from the farm to the consumer's table in order to reduce outbreaks of this bacterial infection and eventually eliminate eggs as a source of it.

product injurious to health or otherwise adulterated as a result of the deviation enters commerce.

Principle 6: *Establish record keeping procedures.*
The HACCP regulation requires that all plants maintain certain documents, including its hazard analysis and written HACCP plan, and records documenting the monitoring of critical control points, critical limits, verification activities, and the handling of processing deviations.

Principle 7: *Establish procedures for verifying the HACCP system is working as intended.*
Validation ensures that the plans do what they were designed to do; that is, they are successful in ensuring the production of safe product. Plants will be required to validate their own HACCP plans. FSIS will not approve HACCP plans in advance, but will review them for conformance with the final rule.

Verification ensures the HACCP plan is adequate, that is, working as intended. Verification procedures may include such activities as review of HACCP plans, CCP records, critical limits, and microbial sampling and analysis. FSIS is requiring that the HACCP plan include verification tasks to be performed by plant personnel. Verification tasks would also be performed by FSIS inspectors. Both FSIS and industry will undertake microbial testing as one of several verification activities.

Source: Food Safety and Inspection Service (FSIS), U.S. Department of Agriculture (USDA), "Key Facts: The Seven HACCP Principles," revised January 1998, http://www.fsis .usda.gov/OA/background/keyhaccp.htm.

These are some examples of the many ways in which the government promotes meat and poultry safety. Agencies continue to improve their methods of regulation and inspection, and provide consumers with educational materials in print and on their Web sites.

Summary

Considering the millions of tons of products that are raised, processed, shipped, sold, prepared, and eaten, producers and government agencies do a good job of providing safe meat and poultry at affordable prices. Experts have said that it may not be humanly possible to guarantee that every single product is free of all bacteria when it reaches the kitchen. According to Michael Pariza, Ph.D., director of the Food Research Institute at the University of Wisconsin, "The USDA has gotten a bum rap. There's no inspection system that anybody could come up with that would guarantee a pathogen-free food supply. There will always be some risk."[234]

Experts see significant progress in reducing meat-borne illnesses since the 1990s, and they expect even more improvements. Through HACCP techniques, safe handling labels, and other approaches, rates of contamination and illness continue to decline. New technology can improve methods of testing for, preventing, and eliminating pathogens.

More Debates

In addition to the topics discussed in previous chapters, concerns are expressed about other aspects of food safety. These include seafood safety, growth hormones in milk, drinking water safety, irradiation, food additives, food labeling, and current regulatory practices, among other concerns.

Seafood Safety

Debates over seafood safety center on pollution, heavy metal toxicity, and food-borne pathogens. Problems can result from hazards in the water itself or during processing and handling. Since conditions vary by season and by region, the EPA maintains a fish advisory information Web site at www.epa.gov/ost/fish.

Each year, about 325,000 people contract illnesses related to eating fish, particularly raw seafood. Infections can occur when sewage reaches fishing waters or people handle fish with soiled hands or tools. In addition to hepatitis and other viruses, bacteria, including salmonella, *Shigella*, and *Vibrio vulnificus*, can contaminate fish. About 10 to 15 people die each year from *Vibrio vulnificus* and many others become ill. Seafood-related illness can also stem from parasites or natural toxins. Scombroid poisoning occurs when certain fish spoil and produce histamine, which can cause nausea, dizziness, headaches, and rashes. In 1999, 26 employees at the World Bank headquarters in Washington, D.C., became ill from scombroid after eating blue marlin from their company's cafeteria.

People also worry about methylmercury, which comes from sediment formed by erosion, undersea volcanoes, industrial pollution, and naturally occurring mercury in the air. This heavy metal is found in certain fish, including tuna, and poses special risks for the developing nervous systems of a fetus or child. After examining research on methylmercury, the EPA advised pregnant women and children to limit their fish consumption. In 2003, the FDA and EPA agreed to warn consumers about fish high in mercury while still encouraging them to include fish in their diets, except for certain species (such as large predatory fish) or any fish caught in waters under a fishing advisory.

Residues of dioxin and other pesticides also have been found in seafood. Lake fish are more likely to contain chemical residues than fish caught in the ocean far from shore. More than 100 chemicals have been found in fishing waters, including PCBs, DDT, chlordane, aldrin, dieldrin, and toxaphene. Some chemicals, including DDT, are now banned, but they remain in lake sediments and persist in the food chain. In 1992, scientists found DDE in 98 percent of the 338 sites, mostly freshwater, that they studied.[235]

Laws set limits on contaminants, including PCBs, mercury, certain pesticides, paralytic shellfish poison, and histamine. Fish inspection falls to state and local officials, but the National

Oceanographic and Atmospheric Administration (NOAA) works with the FDA to close federal waters to fishing in case of oil spills or other events that can make seafood unsafe to eat. Critics think regulatory authority should be more centralized, instead of divided among the FDA, EPA, National Marine Fisheries Service, and local governments.

Yet seafood is often recommended as part of a healthy diet, because it provides protein with less saturated fat than most other flesh foods. It is also a good source of omega-3 fatty acids (EFAs), which are especially high in salmon and certain other varieties. Studies have shown that people who eat at least eight ounces (about 230 grams) of fish weekly have a 50 percent lower risk of heart disease.[236] "On a pound-for-pound basis, seafood is as safe as, if not more safe than, other meat sources," noted Phillip Spiller, director of the FDA's Office of Seafood. "But no food is completely safe, and problems do occur."[237]

In 1997, the FDA launched a program to make seafood safer. It requires processors, repackers, and warehouses in the United States and abroad to follow the Hazard Analysis and Critical Control Point (HACCP) system. HACCP focuses on identifying and preventing hazards rather than relying on random inspections of manufacturing procedures and food samples. Members of the shellfish industry, for example, would examine their methods of growing, harvesting, shucking, packing, and transporting seafood.

Does HAACP go far enough? Critics want agencies to expand their regulating and inspecting functions, set higher standards for sanitation, and improve methods for storage and transportation. They say inspectors should be able to check the storage methods on fishing vessels and immediately ban fishing in polluted waters.

Resources are a problem, however, and some seafood processors have gone for several years without an FDA inspection. "The problem is too much seafood to regulate, too few resources and too little authority [for the agencies involved]," according to

Robert Hahn, former director of legal affairs at the consumer watchdog group Public Voice for Food & Health Policy.[238]

Other safety debates concern bioengineering. Scientists have been testing growth hormones to make fish grow faster and larger. Critics say that GM "superfish" could escape into the wild and monopolize food supplies, thus demolishing smaller fish. They say that companies should be required to obtain approval before they even develop such products. Critics also worry about the potential for allergic reactions when proteins from fish are recombined with proteins from plants or other organisms.

Growth Hormones in Milk

Since 1993, U.S. dairy farmers have been permitted to give cows a synthetic hormone known as recombinant bovine growth hormone (rBGH), scientifically known as bovine somatotropin (rBST). This genetically engineered hormone stimulates cows to produce 10 to 30 percent more milk than normal. Supporters say the hormone is safe, since it is a version of a hormone cows make themselves, and that milk from these cows does not differ from other milk. The FDA reviewed extensive research before approving these hormones and found no significant or toxic side effects in experimental rats that received them. The National Institutes of Health, American Medical Association, American Cancer Society, and American Dietetic Association agree with the FDA. Said Dr. John McNamara, an animal scientist at Washington State University: "Milk is the most tested food you can buy."[239] Milk producers say that banning growth hormones would increase the cost of milk, making this basic food less affordable.

Critics, however, say that rBGH is suspect because the tests were conducted by the company that sells the hormone. "There is a substantial conflict of interest," said Dr. David Kronfeld, an animal scientist at Virginia Polytechnic Institute in Blacksburg.[240] Cows that receive this hormone face a higher risk of udder infection. Antibiotics are used to treat this infection and these residues remain in the milk. Some researchers have found higher levels of insulin-like growth factor (IGF-1) in milk from cows treated with rBGH. They worry that this protein could trigger diabetes in people who are predisposed to that disease. This hormone also encourages cell division and has been linked to breast and other cancers in humans.[241] Reports in scientific journals, including the renowned British medical journal *Lancet*, say that IGF-1 could raise the risk of cancer of the breast, colon, and prostate gland.[242]

Numerous countries, including Japan, Australia, and New Zealand, ban bovine growth hormone. The European Union has placed a moratorium on its use. Canada banned its use in 1999, stating that it hurts animals and was not tested enough to determine all the potential hazards. Canadian scientists referred to studies in which test rats developed antibodies and lesions, and their immune systems were weakened.[243] The FDA countered that the lesions in the rats did not appear to be related to the hormone and that the antibodies in their blood were too low to cause health problems. They noted that natural IGF-1 is already present in milk and the amount added by the hormones is negligible.

What do consumers think? In a 1996 poll, 74 percent of Americans said the hormone might be hazardous and 94 percent wanted mandatory labeling to show its presence in foods.[244] A conflict over labeling led to a lawsuit in 2003. The Monsanto Company sued Oakhurst Dairy in Maine after it put labels on its milk saying that its farmers had pledged not to use artificial growth hormones. The case was settled after Oakhurst agreed to add a statement to its labels saying that the FDA has found "no significant difference in milk from cows treated with artificial growth hormones."[245]

Still, many consumers buy brands of milk with labels saying they are free of artificial growth hormones. Some consumers buy organic milk. Under standards set in 2004, milk cannot be sold as organic unless a year or more goes by after a cow or calf has been treated with antibiotics, growth hormones, or any other drug. Sales of organic milk increased 25 percent between 2004 and 2005.[246] To meet this demand, more dairy farmers have gone organic. Between 1997 and 2003, the number of certified organic milk cows increased by 477 percent.[247]

Drinking Water

All living things depend on water, and humans are no different, using this resource both for hydration and growing food. Surface waters include lakes, rivers, and streams; groundwater refers to underground systems that develop as rainwater and melting snow and ice move through rocks and soil, forming deposits called aquifers. Aquifers supply more than 90 percent of the freshwater in the United States.[248]

Pollution and contamination have plagued water supplies for more than a century. Chemical pollution comes from industry and agriculture, but agriculture contributes the largest amount, including pesticides and nitrates from manures and chemical fertilizers. Pollution also can result from mixing or using chemicals, as well as from spills or losses that occur while storing and transporting them.

Nitrogen reaches water from fertilizer runoff, among other sources. Statistics have shown unsafe levels of nitrate-nitrogen levels in well water and groundwater around the nation. When the U.S. Geological Survey studied wells in 1,663 counties, it found that in 474 of them, 25 percent of the wells had nitrate-nitrogen levels higher than 3 milligrams per liter. In 87 of those 474 counties, 25 percent of wells tested had levels above 10 milligrams per liter, which was the EPA standard for safe drinking water at the time.[249] Over a period of time, drinking water with these levels of nitrate-nitrogen could lead to various health problems, including oxygen deficiency in the blood.

Thousands of wells have been closed around the country because of pesticide contamination from xylene, bentazon, atrazine, simazine, dichloroethylene, and other chemicals the EPA considers toxic. Alachlor, which the EPA has classified as a possible carcinogen, also has been found in U.S. waters.

Chemicals that are purposely added to public water supplies are also controversial. Critics of fluoridation call fluoride a toxic chemical that can cause kidney disease, higher rates of cancer, chromosomal damage, skin conditions, hip fractures, and fertility problems. Supporters of fluoridation, however, say that statistics show a significant decline in the incidence of dental cavities since fluoridation of public water supplies became common after the 1940s. They note that fluoride is a naturally occurring mineral found in various foods and say the amount that is added to water is too small to harm people.[250]

Federal and state programs address issues of water safety, with responsibilities assigned to various agencies and departments. The EPA sets national drinking water standards, with allowable levels for specific contaminants, and it regulates underground injection of liquid waste products into wells. Federal funds can be denied when a project for a highway, building, bridge, or other structure would contaminate an aquifer that is designated as a sole source for drinking water. The EPA also sets standards for bottled water, while the FDA deals with the labeling and safety of bottled water.

Laws relating to drinking water include the Clean Water Act of 1972; the Federal Insecticide, Fungicide, and Rodenticide Act (FIFRA) of 1972; the Safe Drinking Water Act (1974); and the Groundwater Protections Act (1987), which amended federal pesticide laws. People sometimes oppose water safety laws, saying they are unnecessary, can be arbitrary, hamper businesses, and/or encroach upon states' rights. Their opponents, however, want stricter laws that prevent any toxic chemicals from reaching water supplies.

Irradiation of Foods

Since 2000, the USDA's Food Safety and Inspection Service (FSIS) has permitted the use of ionizing radiation for poultry, pork, and beef "for treating refrigerated or frozen uncooked meat, meat by-products, and certain other meat food products to reduce levels of food-borne pathogens and to extend shelf life."[251] The FDA notes that other forms of radiant energy include microwave and infrared radiation, which are used to heat food during cooking, and explains that ionizing radiation "penetrates deeply into food, killing microorganisms without raising the temperature of the food significantly."[252]

Supporters say that irradiation preserves freshness while killing pathogens that can harm consumers. It does not make foods radioactive, as some people fear. It does break down molecules in food, but so does cooking. The USDA, American Medical Association, and World Health Organization consider irradiation to be safe and useful. Janet Riley, a spokesperson for the American Meat Institute, said, "The industry is looking at irradiation as one of many tools in the toolbox."[253] Supporters believe that irradiation makes sense, because pathogens are the most serious food safety problem and can be fatal. They note that critics demand lower levels of bacteria on meat products yet complain about irradiation, which could prevent illnesses and deaths caused by bacterial contamination.

Critics say that irradiation has not been proven safe for consumers. Irradiation breaks down molecular bonds to create new, often unidentifiable, chemicals known as "unique radiolytic products."[254] These chemicals might be toxic to humans or pose other health risks. Testing them properly would require that each substance be identified and then given to laboratory animals in large quantities. Some studies have reported long-term heart and kidney damage in laboratory animals that ate irradiated foods.[255] Alternatives to irradiation include hot water sprays, nontoxic detergents, and sprays made from citric acid or acetic acids. The meat industry could choose these methods or, better still, improve their production methods to prevent contamination.

Since 1966, the FDA has required that irradiated foods be labeled. An identifying symbol—the radura—was added in 1986. When the word "irradiated" is not part of the product name, the labels must include the words "treated with radiation" or "treated by irradiation."[256]

Food Additives

Some commonly used food additives—for example, MSG, artificial sweeteners, nitrates, and artificial colors—arouse concern. Additives are used to preserve foods, enhance flavor, texture, and/or appearance, or add sweetness with fewer calories, among other reasons.

MSG—monosodium glutamate—has been widely used since the 1970s. This flavor-enhancing substance is classified as an excitotoxin, a group of chemicals that affect the body's neurological system. Critics say MSG use is linked to numerous diseases, symptoms, and complaints, including tumors, heart disease, asthma, neurological and emotional disorders, and headaches. People who are sensitive to MSG can experience swelling of the throat and tongue, racing heartbeat, dizziness, joint pain, skin disorders, burning sensations, and/or gastrointestinal issues.[257] Studies have shown that in animals, MSG can cause brain lesions by killing brain cells.[258]

Consumers also wonder about additives that make food look better, fresher, or different, a practice that is facilitated by new technology. Some of these ingredients are not required on labels, while others are not detectable because they receive general names such as "flavor" or "coloring" that do not describe exactly what was added.

In 1938, the FDA began to certify dyes that could be legally used in foods, but some critics think that even approved food dyes can be unsafe and carcinogenic. Consumer groups complained about red dye #3, a colorant that was widely used for maraschino cherries, alcoholic beverages, and canned fruits, saying that it was a possible carcinogen. In 1990, the FDA did ban most uses of this chemical, based on studies that very high amounts could cause cancer in laboratory animals.[259] The FDA added that it considered these risks quite small—about 1 in 100,000 over a 70-year lifetime.[260]

Coloring agents have become increasingly common in an era when foods are shipped long distances and are often canned, bottled, or packaged—not fresh. Titanium dioxide, a mineral that is also used in house paints, gives some canned cake frostings and frozen dairy whipped creams their bright white color. Sodium ascorbate, an antioxidant and color stabilizer, is added to bacon and various cold cuts to make them look redder. A pigment called canthaxanthin may be added to chicken feed so that the bird's skin turns more golden. Egg producers can also add dye in the form of xanthophyll and carotenoids to chicken feed. This dye is absorbed and metabolized and ends up in the yolk, imparting a richer yellow-orange hue. These products come with charts showing how much pigment is needed to achieve a certain color.

Astaxanthin and canthaxanthin may be added to the feed of farm-raised salmon to turn their gray-toned flesh a red-pink or red-orange color. This makes them look more like wild salmon, which are naturally dark in color because of the food they eat. After reviewing studies that showed high levels of these chemicals can harm eyesight, the European Union limited the amounts that can be given to salmon. In 2004, a law firm in Seattle, Washington, filed a class action suit against two large grocery chains in Washington state and California, stating that they had a duty to tell consumers that their farm-raised salmon were dyed. Although that case was dismissed, consumers became more aware of these dyes and some stores voluntarily put the phrase "color added" on their salmon labels.

Carbon monoxide is sometimes added to red meats to help them retain their color longer. Although this practice does not seem to harm human health, it poses other dangers by disguising the actual age of the meat. No laws require sellers to inform consumers about the addition of carbon monoxide, so buyers may not know their meat was treated in order to look fresher longer. Critics say consumers have the right to know exactly what they are buying and eating.

More Information for Consumers?

Although important labeling laws were enacted in recent decades, critics say these labels don't give consumers enough information about the origins and contents of foods. They say that current laws give food product companies too much discretion in terms of what they list and how they list it. One example is a red dye that comes from female cochineal beetles and is used in some candies, yogurt, and other products. Companies may list this ingredient with the general term "artificial color" or call it "carmine" or "cochineal extract." A small percentage of consumers are allergic to carmine, and these people need specific information for safety reasons. Vegetarians also seek this information so they can avoid products that contain insect parts or extracts.[261]

One contentious area involves labeling genetically modified (GM) foods. Laws do not require companies to inform consumers, saying this is impractical and unnecessary. In a 1993 publication, the FDA stated that labeling is required for information that is "material" and to "avoid false or misleading statements." It maintains the position that "the method by which a plant is developed by a plant breeder is not material information in the sense of the law."[262]

More recently, country of origin labeling has sparked heated debates. Under the 2002 Farm Bill, fresh beef, pork, and lamb must bear country-of-origin labels (COOL), while processed meat products are exempt. This means labeling meat to show where the animal used to produce it was born, raised, or slaughtered, whether inside or outside the United States. A label on ground beef, for example, might show that the cow was born and raised in Canada or Mexico and then processed in the United States. Labels on ground meat might show that the mixture came from more than one country. Consumer groups want such laws because about 20 percent of beef sold in the United States comes from cattle born elsewhere. They say sellers should not be able to sell foreign-grown meat or mixtures of foreign and domestic meat for the same price at which they sell domestic meat.

Critics of COOL laws say these regulations place unfair and impractical burdens on meat producers, which could lead to higher meat prices. The USDA has estimated that the labeling program could cost the industry $1.9 billion. If those costs are passed on to consumers, an average U.S. household will pay about 40 cents per week more for their beef.[263] The American Meat Institute, which opposes the law, says that extra costs would arise due to the reconfigurations needed to track the source of the animals and raw materials, extra storage to segregate products, more record-keeping, and the labels themselves. Meat producers also say these laws are unfair because they do not affect poultry.

The COOL law was supposed to be implemented in 2004 but Congress postponed it twice. As of 2007, it was slated for implementation on September 30, 2008. Members of the meat industry continue to say that the COOL law should be repealed.[264]

New Approaches to Food Safety?

Federal food safety programs came under increasing scrutiny as 2006 brought new cases of food-borne death and illness. A new outbreak of *E. coli* caused more than 300 people in at least a half-dozen states to become ill. Investigators traced the probable source of infection—green onions—to Taco Bell restaurants in New Jersey, New York, Pennsylvania, Delaware, South Carolina, and Utah. It took about two and one-half weeks to trace this probable cause—too long, say critics. Inspectors pointed out that their work is painstaking and difficult because they must inspect thousands of food outlets. Within a few days, tainted food items can reach several states. By the time one patient is identified, others are already sick.

Then, in May 2007, consumers learned that several popular brands of pet food were contaminated with a chemical that originated from China. Thousands of cats and dogs became sick and some died. This incident highlighted the problems that can occur when raw materials for foods are imported from countries that lack strict food safety laws and policies. To reduce costs, however, more American companies have been importing materials that go into foods.

Critics say that new approaches and specific planning are needed to adequately address changing risks and circumstances, including the threat of terrorism. "Our system for inspecting food and drug imports into the USA is woefully outdated, designed to regulate a mostly domestic industry, not to deal with a globalized world," wrote Scott Gottlieb, who served as deputy commissioner at the FDA from 2005 to 2007. Gottlieb says that the FDA must "be able to better identify and prioritize risks from imported products all along their life cycle, and not just at the border."[265] To monitor imports, safety agencies must be able to confirm that foreign companies follow health and safety requirements while food products are being produced, stored, and shipped. Agencies also need to be able to identify products that pose high risks.

Lawmakers have proposed a new kind of federal agency that would focus squarely on food safety. In 2006, senators Charles Schumer and Hillary Rodham Clinton, both Democrats from New York, sponsored legislation to create a unified Food Safety Agency. Schumer said that recent events, including the contaminated spinach and the recall of 5,200 pounds of ground beef, were "a wake-up call to get our food safety house in order because right now it's in pure disarray."[266] The bill addressed the confusion that can arise because of the way responsibility for food safety is currently dispersed. Putting one agency in charge, said Schumer, can eliminate the kinds of problems that occur when various agencies are "butting heads."[267] Under this legislation, companies would also be required to code products to make it easier and faster to track products after an outbreak of food-borne illness. Other provisions would improve prevention and inspection techniques and give the FDA authority to recall foods.[268]

Will the U.S. food safety system be dramatically reorganized? Will stricter laws be implemented and enforced? Critics complain that efforts to improve food safety historically run into resistance from powerful food industry lobbying. "Food producers resist the attempts of government agencies to institute control measures, and major food industries oppose pathogen control measures by every means at their disposal," says author Marion Nestle. "They lobby Congress and federal agencies, challenge regulations in court, and encourage local obstruction of safety enforcement."[269] For their part, members of the food industry point out that they are committed to providing safe foods and that they consistently manage to deliver diverse foods at affordable prices.

Summary

As these chapters have shown, debates over food safety are complex and not easily resolved. They often involve competing political, economic, and social interests, as well as conflicting scientific reports or different interpretations of those reports. Arguments on various sides may also reflect people's values and sensibilities, since food can be an emotional subject. Americans continue to face many challenges as they debate these important issues and aim to make the food supply as safe as possible.

Introduction: A Safe Food Supply?

1 Andrew Bridges, "Spinach Bacteria Linked to Cattle Ranch," *Washington Post,* October 12, 2006, http://www .washingtonpost.com/wp-dyn/content/ article/2006/10/12/AR2006101201181 .html.

2 "Tainted Spinach Traced to California Ranch," *Science Daily,* March 24, 2007, http://www.sciencedaily.com/upi/ index.php?feed=Science&article= UPI-1-20070324-14221600-bc-us- spinach.xml.

3 Dan Hager, "E. Coli Found in Vegetables," *Vegetarian Times,* July 1995, 14.

4 Centers for Disease Control and Prevention, "Update: Multistate Outbreak of *Escherichia coli* 0157:H7 Infections from Hamburgers—Western United States, 1992–1993," *Morbidity and Mortality Weekly Report,* April 16, 1993. For further discussion, see: B.P. Bell, et. al., "A Multistate Outbreak of Escherichia Coli O157:H7-Associated Bloody Diarrhea and Hemolytic Uremic Syndrome from Hamburgers: The Washington Experience," *Journal of the American Medical Association,* November 2, 1994, 1349–1353; and Sandra B. Eskin, Nancy Donley, Donna Rosenbaum, and Karen Taylor Mitchell, *Why Are People Still Dying From Contaminated Food?* Report from Safe Tables Our Priority (STOP), February 2003, http://www.safetables .org/pdf/STOP_Report.pdf.

5 U.S. Centers for Disease Control, "Outbreaks of *Salmonella enteritidis* Gastroenteritis—California, 1993," *Morbidity and Mortality Weekly Report* 42(41), October 22, 1993.

6 David Schardt and Stephen Schmidt, "Keeping Food Safe," *Nutrition Health Newsletter,* April 1995, 4.

7 U.S. Centers for Disease Control, "Preliminary FoodNet Data on the Incidence of Foodborne Illnesses," April 19, 2002, http://www.cdc.gov/mmwr/preview/ mmwrhtml/mm5115a3.htm.

8 *Ibid.*

9 Quoted in Peter Pringle, *Food, Inc.* (New York: Simon & Schuster, 2003), 110.

10 Jack Kittredge, "Big Ag Fights Back," *Natural Farmer,* Winter 1999–2000, 14.

11 Cited in *U.S. v. Lexington Mill & Elevator Co.*, 232 U.S. 399 (1914).

12 "Federal Food, Drug, and Cosmetics Act of 1938," U.S. Food and Drug Administration, http://www.fda.gov/opacom/ laws/fdcact/fdctoc.htm.

13 Rachel Carson, *Silent Spring* (London: Readers Union, 1964).

14 Gary Null, *Clearer, Cleaner, Safer, Greener: A Blueprint for Detoxifying Your Environment* (New York: Random House, 1990), 103.

15 *Ibid.*

16 Quoted in Sharon Begley and Mary Hager, "A Guide to the Grocery," *Newsweek,* March 27, 1989, 18.

17 Gallup poll accompanying Begley and Hager, "A Guide to the Grocery," *Newsweek,* March 27, 1989, 22.

18 Quoted in Pesticide Management and Education Program/Cornell University, "Proposed EPA/plaintiff agreement for carcinogens in food," http://pmep.cce .cornell.edu/issues/epa-agree-carcin.html.

19 Quoted in John H. Cushman, Jr., "E.P.A. Settles Suit and Agrees to Move Against 36 Pesticides," *New York Times,* October 13, 1994, A-24.

20 *Ibid.*

21 "The Enforcer: Doctor, Lawyer, FDA Chief," *Newsweek.* May 27, 1991, 50.

22 Nancy Donley, speaking to Congress, February 15, 1995.

23 U.S. Environmental Protection Agency, "Pesticide Reregistration Facts." Available online. URL: http://www.epa.gov/ pesticides/factsheets/factshee.htm.

24 Marion Nestle, *Safe Food: Bacteria, Biotechnology, and Bioterrorism* (Berkeley: University of California Press, 2004), 57.

Point: Using Pesticides and Other Chemicals in Food Production Poses Health Risks for Consumers

25 National Resources Defense Council (NRDC), *Intolerable Risk: Pesticides in Our Children's Food* (Washington, D.C.: NRDC, 1989).

26 Al Heier, "EPA Accelerates Process to Cancel Daminozide [Alar] Uses on Apples; Extends Tolerance," *EPA Environmental News* [press release] February 1, 1989. See also: Philip Shabecoff, "Hazard Reported in Apple Chemical," *New York Times*, February 2, 1989, 23.

27 Begley and Hager, "A Guide to the Grocery," 20.

28 R.J. Smith, "Hawaiian milk contamination creates alarm, a sour response by regulators," *Science* 217 (1982): 137–140.

29 Null, *Clearer, Cleaner, Safer, Greener*, 113.

30 "Feds: Tainted Cereal Safe," *Vegetarian Times*, August 1995, 19.

31 Null, p. 113. See also: K.L. Davis, J.A. Savage, and P.A. Berger, "Possible Organophosphate Induced Parkinsonism," *Journal of Mental Nervous Disorder* 66 (1978): 222–225; R.D. Hinsdill, D.L. Couch, and R.S. Speirs, "Immunosuppression Induced by Dioxin (TCDD) in Feed," *Journal of Environmental Toxicology* 4 (1980): 401; Sheila Hoar, et al., "Agricultural Herbicide Use and Risk of Lymphoma and Soft-Tissue Sarcoma," *Journal of the American Medical Association* (September 5, 1986): 1141–1147.

32 Susan Gilbert, "America Tackles the Pesticide Crisis," *New York Times Magazine*, October 8, 1989, 51.

33 "List of Chemicals Evaluated for Carcinogenic Potential," Washington, D.C.: U.S. Environmental Protection Agency, 1990.

34 Quoted in Begley and Hager, "A Guide to the Grocery," 20.

35 See E.G. Vallianatos, "America's Farm Workers Still Toil in Fields of Danger," *Baltimore Sun*, February 22, 2007, http://www.organicconsumers.org/articles/article_4750.cfm. See also: "Study Shows Pesticides are Poisoning Farm Workers & Their Families," *Agribusiness Examiner*, February 2, 2005.

36 Cited in Michael F. Jacobson, Lisa Y. Lefferts, and Anne Witte Garland, *Safe Food: Eating Wisely in a Risky World* (Los Angeles: Living Planet Press, 1991), 48.

37 Conger Beasley Jr., "Of Pollution and Poverty," *Buzzword: The Environmental Journal* (May-June 1990): 40, 42.

38 U.S. Environmental Protection Agency, "Pesticides and Child Safety," February 2004, http://www.epa.gov/pesticides/factsheets/childsaf.htm.

39 Frank Falck, Jr., et al., "Pesticides and Polychlorinated Biphenyl Residues in Human Breast Lipids and Their Relation to Breast Cancer," *Archives of Environmental Health* 47, no. 2 (March/April, 1992): 143–146.

40 Null, *Clearer, Cleaner, Safer, Greener*, 116–117. See also: "Belgian Butter Latest Food Banned in Dioxin Scandal," June 7, 1999, http://www.cnn.com/WORLD/europe/9906/07/eu.food.

41 Mothers and Others For Pesticide Limits, *Pesticides in Children's Food* (Washington, D.C.: National Resources Defense Council, 1989).

42 Ben McKelway, *Guess What's Coming to Dinner: Contaminants in Our Food* (Washington, D.C.: Center for Science in the Public Interest), 6.

43 Karen Matthews, "NY Sen. Schumer says loose fed oversight puts food supply at risk," Newsday.com, October 8, 2006.

44 McKelway, *Guess What's Coming to Dinner*, 8.

45 USFDA Center for Food Safety and Applied Nutrition, "FDA Food Recall Policies," June 2002, http://www.cfsan.fda.gov/~lrd/recall2.html.

46 Sheila Kaplan, "The Food Chain Gang," *Common Cause Magazine*, September/October 1987, 12.

47 Beyond Pesticides National Coalition, "EPA Completes Pesticide Review—Are Our Children Better Protected?" August 7, 2006, http://www.beyondpesticides.org/news/daily_news_archive/2006/08_07_06.htm.

48 Sheila Kaplan, "The Food Chain Gang."

49 See David Pimentel, et al., "Environmental and Economic Impacts of Reducing U.S. Agricultural Pesticide Use," in *CRC Handbook of Pest Management in Agriculture*, ed. David Pimentel, 679–718 (London: CRC Press, 1990).

50 Jacobson, Lefferts, and Garland, *Safe Food*, 48.

51 McKelway, *Guess What's Coming To Dinner*, 6.

52 Null, *Clearer, Cleaner, Safer, Greener*, 104.

53 The Common Sense Environmental Fund, "Soil Erosion," http://www .csshome.com/sustainableagriculture .htm.

54 Carson, *Silent Spring*, 36.

55 See: Margaret Reeves and Terra Murphy, "Farmworker Women and Pesticides in California's Central Valley," Report from the Pesticide Action Network North America, February 2003, http:// www.panna.org/resources/documents/ CVEnglish2-20.pdf. See also: National Resources Defense Council, "Drinking Water Contamination," Ch. 7 in *Our Children at Risk*, http://www.nrdc.org/ health/kids/ocar/chap7.asp.

56 Jacobson, Lefferts, and Garland, *Safe Food*, 46.

57 Joan Goldstein, *Demanding Clean Food and Water* (New York: Plenum Publishing, 1990), 146–147.

58 Food, Agriculture, Conservation, and Trade Act of 1990 (FACTA), Public Law 101-624, Title XVI, Subtitle A, Section 1603 (Washington, D.C.: Government Printing Office, 1990).

59 Jules Pretty, "Feeding the World?" *SPLICE* 4, no. 6 (August-September 1998), http://ngin.tripod.com/article2 .htm

60 Gilbert, "America Tackles the Pesticide Crisis," 25.

61 Harold Faber, "Farmer's Apples Aren't Pretty and She Likes Them That Way," *New York Times*, October 6, 1989.

62 Garth Youngberg, *Report and Recommendation on Organic Farming* (Washington, D.C.: United States Department of Agriculture, 1980).

63 Goldstein, *Demanding Clean Food and Water*, 168–169.

64 Gallup poll accompanying "Begley and Hager, "A Guide to the Grocery," 22.

65 Quoted in Steven Shapin, "Paradise Sold," *New Yorker*, May 15, 2006, http:// www.newyorker.com/archive/2006/05/ 15/060515crat_atlarge.

66 "Study: Shoppers Loading Up On Organic Foods," *Denver Business Journal*, September 27, 2006, http://www .bizjournals.com/denver/stories/ 2006/09/25/daily43.html.

67 Virginia Worthington, "Effect of Agricultural Methods on Nutritional Quality: A Comparison of Organic With Conventional Crops," *Alternative Therapies* 4 (1998): 58–69.

68 Worthington, "Nutritional Quality of Organic Vs. Conventional Fruits, Vegetables, and Grains," *Journal of Alternative and Complementary Medicine* 7, no. 2 (2001): 161–173.

69 Carol Browner, speaking to American Wildlife Association, June 6, 2003.

70 Quoted in Richard Rhodes, "Organic Farms: Agriwisdom," *New York Times*, November 24, 1989.

Counterpoint: Using Approved Chemicals Is Safe and Offers Important Benefits

71 Judith E. Foulke, "FDA Reports on Pesticides in Foods," *FDA Consumer*, June 1993.

72 Jane E. Brody, "Chemicals in Food? A Panel of Experts Finds Little Danger," *New York Times*, February 16, 1996, A1, http://query.nytimes.com/gst/fullpage .html?sec=health&res=9A0DE6D71239 F935A25751C0A960958260.

73 Quoted in Sam Libby, "Growers Worry About Alar-Free Apples," *New York Times*, September 17, 1989.

74 Quoted in Faber, "Farmer's Apples Aren't Pretty and She Likes Them That Way."

75 Quoted in Timothy Egan, "Apple Growers Bruised and Bitter After Alar Scare," *New York Times*, July 9, 1991.

76 Quoted in Faber, "Farmer's Apples Aren't Pretty and She Likes Them That Way."

77 Brody, "Chemicals in Food?"

78 Egan, "Apple Growers Bruised and Bitter After Alar Scare."

79 Quoted in Jessica Snyder Sachs, "Hidden Dangers in Your Food and Water," *McCalls*, August 1994, 46.

80 Bruce N. Ames, Renae Magaw, and Lois Swirsky Gold, "Ranking Possible Carcinogenic Hazards," *Science,* April 17, 1987, 271–280.

81 See Lois Swirsky Gold, Thomas H. Slone, Neela B. Manley, and Bruce N. Ames, *Misconceptions about the Causes of Cancer,* The Fraser Institute. Vancouver: British Columbia, Canada, 2002.

82 Dennis Avery, *Saving the Planet With Pesticides and Plastic: The Environmental Triumph of High-Yield Farming* (Washington, D.C.: Hudson Institute, 2000), 408.

83 "Study Finds No Increased Risk of Breast Cancer from DDT and PCBs," *Harvard University Gazette,* October 30, 1997, http://hno.harvard.edu/gazette/1997/10.30/StudyFindsNoInc.html.

84 *Ibid.*

85 Brody, "Chemicals in Food?"

86 Anthony Trewavas, "Urban Myths of Organic Farming," *Nature,* March 22, 2001, 409–410.

87 Begley and Hager, "A Guide to the Grocery," 20.

88 World Cancer Research Fund, *Food, Nutrition, and the Prevention of Cancer: A Global Perspective* (Washington, D.C.: American Institute for Cancer Research, 1997).

89 Commission on Life Sciences, *Diet and Health: Implications for Reducing Chronic Disease* (Washington, D.C.: National Academy Press, 1989).

90 National Research Council, *Carcinogens and Anticarcinogens in the Human Diet: A Comparison of Naturally Occurring and Synthetic Substances* (Washington, D.C.: National Academy Press, 1996), 309.

91 Quoted in Gloria Bucco, "Our Farmlands at Risk," *Delicious,* April 1994, 20.

92 Joseph D. Rosen, "Much Ado About Alar," *Issues in Science and Technology,* Fall 1990, 86, http://courses.washington.edu/alisonta/pbaf590/pdf/Rosen_Alar.pdf.

93 EPA, "Prevention, Pesticides and Toxic Substances," September 1999, http://www.epa.gov/oppts.

94 Donna U. Vogt, CRS Report for Congress: "The Delaney Clause Effects on Pesticide Policy," Congressional Research Service (CRS) Report: 95-514, http://www.ncseonline.org/NLE/CRSreports/Pesticides/pest-1.cfm.

95 Judith E. Foulke, "FDA Reports on Pesticides in Foods," *FDA Consumer,* June 1993, http://www.cfsan.fda.gov/~lrd/pesticid.html.

96 See: U.S. Food and Drug Administration, Center for Food Safety and Applied Nutrition, "Food Labeling and Nutrition," http://www.cfsan.fda.gov/label.html. See also: "Consumer Nutrition and Health Information," http://www.cfsan.fda.gov/~dms/lab-cons.html.

97 See: FDA, "Food Labeling Consumer and Nutrition Information," http://www.fda.gov/ola/2003/counterterrorism1119.html.

98 Quoted in Keith Schneider, "Food Industry Is Testing for Toxics To Reassure Consumers on Crops," *New York Times,* March 27, 1989, B12.

99 USDA Food Safety and Inspection Service (FSIS), "Molds On Food—Are They Dangerous?" USDA Fact Sheet, http://www.fsis.usda.gov/Fact_Sheets/Molds_On_Food/index.asp.

100 Trewavas, "Is Organic Food Really Safe?"

101 Avery, *Saving the Planet With Pesticides and Plastic,* 187.

102 See: National Center for Policy Analysis (NCPA), "Is Organic Food Really Safer and Healthier?" September 20, 2004, http://www.ncpa.org/sub/dpd/index.php?Article_ID=629. See also: Dave Juday, "Are Organic Foods Really Better For You?" BridgeNews Service, Hudson Institute Center for Global Food Issues, February 11, 2000, http://www.cgfi.org/materials/articles/2000/feb_11_00.htm.

103 Trewavas, "Is Organic Food Really Safe?"

104 Former Secretary of Agriculture Earl Butz speaking to the Institute of Food

Technologists in Anaheim, California, June 6, 1976.

105 Shapin, "Paradise Sold."

106 "California Reports on Methyl Bromide," *Agrichemical and Environmental News*, March 1996. See also: SB 1371 Senate Bill Analysis, February 21, 1996.

107 Quoted in Anita Manning, "USDA Gives Bite to Organic Label," *USA Today*, November 15, 2002, http://www.usatoday.com/news/nation/2002-10-15-organic-usat_x.htm.

108 *Ibid.*

109 See Melissa Healy, "Behind the Organic Label: As the industry grows, skeptics are challenging the health claims," September 6, 2004.

110 Trewavas, "Is Organic Food Really Safe?"

111 Shapin, "Paradise Sold."

112 Avery, *Saving the Planet With Pesticides and Plastic*, 12.

113 *Ibid.*

114 *Ibid.*

115 Avery, 193.

116 Stanley W. Trimble, "Decreased Rates of Alluvial Sediment Storage in the Coon Creek Basin, Wisconsin, 1975–93," *Science,* August 1999, 1187–1189.

117 Rosen, "Much Ado About Alar."

118 Quoted in Egan, "Apple Growers Bruised and Bitter After Alar Scare."

Point: Genetically Modified Foods Can Be Dangerous for Consumers and the Environment

119 See Nestle, *Safe Food*, 172–176; John C. Avise, *The Hope, Hype, and Reality of Genetic Engineering: Remarkable Stories from Agriculture, Industry, Medicine, and the Environment* (New York: Oxford University Press, 2004), 37.

120 Karl J. Mogel and Wolfgang Rougle, "Should genetic engineering be banned?" *The California Aggie*, http://media.www.californiaaggie.com/media/storage/paper981/news/2005/05/18/Features/Mogel.Vs.Rougle.Should.Genetic.Engineering.Be.Banned-1320600.shtml. See also: Andrew Pollack, "Study Raises Doubts

About Allergy to Genetic Corn," *New York Times*, November 10, 2003.

121 Pringle, *Food, Inc.*, 2.

122 *Ibid.*

123 C. James, "Global Status of Commercialized Biotech/gm Crops," ISAAA Briefs, No. 34, International Service for the Acquisition of Agri-Biotech Applications (ISAAA), 2005.

124 Kathleen Hart, *Eating in the Dark: America's Experiment with Genetically Engineered Food* (New York: Pantheon Books, 2002), 6.

125 "Genetically Modified Foods in the United States," Pew Initiative on Food and Biotechnology: Fact Sheet, August 2004, http://pewagbiotech.org/resources/factsheets/display.php3?FactsheetID=2. See also: Interview with Robert B. Horsch by Sasha Nemecek, "Does the World Need GM Foods? Yes," *Scientific American Reports*, March 14, 2007, 38.

126 Sasha Nemecek, interview with Margaret Mellon, "Does the World Need GM Foods?" *Scientific American Reports*, March 14, 2007, 39.

127 See Ralph Nader, foreword to Martin Teitel and Kimberly A. Wilson, *Genetically Engineered Food: Changing the Nature of Nature* (Rochester, Vt.: Park Street Press, 2001), ix.

128 *Ibid.*, 13.

129 Michael Antoniou, "GM Foods: Current Tests Are Inadequate Protection," *London Sunday Independent*, February 21, 1999.

130 Quoted in Pringle, *Food, Inc.*, 97.

131 Mae-Wan Ho, "Special Safety Concerns of Transgenic Agriculture and Related Issues," Institute of Science in Society, *ISIS News* 3, 1999.

132 Hart, *Eating in the Dark*, 15.

133 See Lennart Hardell, M.D., Ph.D., and Mikael Eriksson, M.D., Ph.D., "A Case-Control Study of Non-Hodgkin Lymphoma and Exposure to Pesticides," *Cancer*, March 15, 1999.

134 Hart, *Eating in the Dark*, 19.

135 Nemecek, "Does the World Need GM Foods?"

136 Nemecek, "Does the World Need GM Foods?"

137 Nestle, *Safe Food*, 149.

138 Hart, *Eating in the Dark*, 27.

139 Pringle, *Food, Inc.*, 33.

140 Council for Responsible Genetics, "The Genetic Bill of Rights," http://www.gene-watch.org/programs/bill-of-rights/bill-of-rights-text.html.

141 Pringle, *Food, Inc.*, 33–34.

142 Quoted in Genetic Resources Action International (GRAIN), "Briefing: Engineering Solutions to Malnutrition," March 2000, http://www.grain.org/briefings/?id=142.

143 Quoted in Teitel and Wilson, *Genetically Engineered Food*, 31.

144 Nemecek, "Does the World Need GM Foods?"

145 "Open Letter by the Independent Scientists to be read at Joint International GMO Opposition Day," April 8, 2006, http://www.organicconsumers.org/ge/openletter122105.cfm.

Counterpoint: Genetically Modified Foods Are Safe for Consumption and Have Other Advantages

146 Pringle, *Food, Inc.*, 29.

147 Interview with Robyn Williams, "Genetically Engineered Crops," *Ockham's Razor*, Radio National-Australian Broadcasting Corporation, September 9, 1999, http://abc.net.au/rn/science/ockham/stories/s54399.htm.

148 "Micronutrient Deficiencies: Vitamin A Deficiency," World Health Organization (WHO), http://www.who.int/nutrition/topics/vad/en. See also: Genetic Resources Action International (GRAIN), "Briefing: Engineering Solutions to Malnutrition," March 2000, http://www.grain.org/briefings/?id=142.

149 Interview with Williams, "Genetically Engineered Crops."

150 Interview with FDA's Jim Maryanski, "Genetically Engineered Foods: Fears and Facts," *FDA Consumer*, January-February 1993.

151 Beth Fitzgerald, "Jersey Lab Splices Veggie Gene," *Sunday Star-Ledger*, July 4, 1993, Section 3, 6.

152 Interview with Maryanski "Genetically Engineered Foods: Fears and Facts."

153 Quoted in Hart, *Eating in the Dark*, 37.

154 Quoted in Hart, 23.

155 Quoted in Nemecek, "Does the World Need GM Foods? Yes."

156 Fitzgerald, "Jersey Lab Splices Veggie Gene," 5, 6.

157 Linda Bren, "Genetic Engineering: The Future of Foods?" *FDA Consumer*, November/December 2003, http://www.fda.gov/fdac/features/2003/603_food.html.

158 Bill Hord, "Researcher Seeks New Ways to Feed Hungry World," *Omaha World-Herald*, April 11, 2007, http://www.omaha.com/index.php?u_page=1208&u_sid=2363093.

159 *Ibid.*

160 Florence Wambugu, "Biotechnology: Protesters Don't Grasp Africa's Need," *Los Angeles Times*, November 11, 2001, M-1.

161 Ingo Potrykus, "Golden Rice and Beyond," *Plant Physiology*, March 2001, 157–161.

162 *Ibid.*

163 Quoted in Nemecek, "Does the World Need GM Foods? Yes."

Point: The Regulatory Process Does Not Protect Consumers from the Hazards of Meat and Poultry Production

164 See: Nestle, *Safe Food*, 251; Associated Press, "Feds fight broad testing for mad cow disease," May 29, 2007, http://www.msnbc.msn.com/id/18924801.

165 Discussed in Sheldon Rampton and John Stauber, *Mad Cow U.S.A.: Could the Nightmare Happen Here?* (Monroe, Maine: Common Courage Press, 1997). See also: transcript of Oprah Winfrey broadcast, available online at http://www.vegsource.com/lyman/oprah_transcript.htm.

166 Rampton and Stauber, 215.

167 Cathy Booth Thomas, "How Now Mad Cow?" *Time*, January 3, 2004, http://www.time.com/time/magazine/article/0,9171,1101040112-570218,00.html.

168 Steve Striffler, *Chicken: The Dangerous Transformation of America's Favorite Food* (New Haven: Yale University Press, 2005), 162.

169 Cited in Striffler, 163.

170 Caroline Smith DeWaal, J.D., "Playing Chicken: The Human Cost of Inadequate Regulation of the Poultry Industry," Center for Science in the Public Interest, March 1996, 5.

171 Striffler, *Chicken*, 162.

172 T.W. Hennessy, C.W. Hedburg, I. Slutsker, et al., "A National Outbreak of Salmonella Enteriditis Infection in Ice Cream," *New England Journal of Medicine* (1996): 1281–1286.

173 Marian Burros, "Experts Concerned About Return of Deadly Bacteria in Cold Cuts," *New York Times*, March 14, 1999, 23.

174 *Modern Meat*, produced and directed by Doug Hamilton (PBS, April 18, 2002).

175 Christopher Cook, *Diet for a Dead Planet: Big Business and the Coming Food Crisis.* New York: the New Press, 2006, 57.

176 Jeremy H. Rees, et al., "Campylobacter Jejuni Infection and Guillain-Barre Syndrome," *New England Journal of Medicine* (November 23, 1995): 1374–1379.

177 Cook, 58.

178 "Dirty Birds," *Consumer Reports*, January 2007, http://www.consumerreports.org/cro/food/chicken-safety-1-07/overview/0107_chick_ov.htm edition. See also: Salynn Boyles, "Most Chicken Harbors Harmful Bacteria," WebMD Medical News, December 4, 2006, http://www.medicinenet.com/script/main/art.asp?articlekey=77924.

179 Cook, 64. See also: Union of Concerned Scientists, "Hogging It: Estimates of Antimicrobial Abuse in Livestock," press release, 2001, http://go.ucsusa.org/publications/report.cfm?publicationID=147.

180 Union of Concerned Scientists, "What's in the Meat You Eat?" October 2003, http://www.ucsusa.org/publications/greentips/1003-whats-in-the-meat-you-eat.html.

181 "Dirty Birds," *Consumer Reports.*

182 McKelway, *Guess What's Coming to Dinner*, 29.

183 Cook, 65; see also Michael Pollan, "Power Steer," *New York Times*, March 31, 2001.

184 McKelway, *Guess What's Coming to Dinner*, 22.

185 *Ibid.*, 22–23.

186 *Ibid.*, 26.

187 Nichole Monroe Bell, "Critics Want Tighter Rules on Animal Feed," *Charlotte Observer*, April 30, 2007, http://www.charlotte.com/217/story/104287.html.

188 Union of Concerned Scientists, "Livestock and Meat Marketing Labels Fall Short," March 27, 2003, http://www.ucsusa.org/food_and_environment/sustainable_food/usda-meat-marketing-labels-fall-short.html.

189 Cook, 57.

190 *Modern Meat.*

191 Donald D. Stull, Michael J. Broadway, and David Griffith, eds., *Any Way You Cut It: Meat Processing and Small-Town America* (Lawrence: University Press of Kansas, 1995), 46.

192 Government Accountability Office (GAO), Report to the Ranking Minority Member, Committee on Health, Education, Labor, and Pensions, U.S. Senate, "Workplace Safety and Health: Safety in the Meat and Poultry Industry, While Improving, Could Be Further Strengthened," January 2005.

193 2005 Human Rights Watch Report, cited in Striffler, *Chicken*, 129.

194 Cook, 62.

195 Richard Behar and Michael Kramer, "Something Smells Fowl," *Time*, October 17, 1994, 43.

196 Cited in Nestle, *Safe Food*, 76.

197 Schardt and Schmidt, "Keeping Food Safe," 6.

198 Quoted in Schardt and Schmidt, 6.

199 Cook, 59–60. See also: Stan Grossfeld, "Animal Waste Emerging as U.S. Problem," *Boston Globe*, September 21, 1998.

200 Cook, 61.

201 Nestle, *Safe Food*, 87–88.

202 Senator Tom Harkin, "Harkin calls for audit of nation's food safety system," press release, April 25, 2007, http://harkin.senate.gov/news.cfm?id=273076.

203 Keesia Wirt, "America Has Cheapest, Safest Food Supply in the World: Another AG Myth," originally published in *The Agribusiness Examiner*, April 2, 2004, available online at http://www.organicconsumers.org/foodsafety/foodmyth040504.cfm.

Counterpoint: Modern Production Methods and Regulatory Procedures Provide Consumers With Quality Meats

204 Quoted in Libby Quaid, "U.S. Investigates Possible Case of Mad Cow Disease," Associated Press, March 11, 2006.

205 *Ibid.*

206 Thomas, "How Now Mad Cow."

207 Quoted in U.S. Department of Health and Human Services (HHS), "Fewer Americans Suffer From Foodborne Illnesses as Food Safety Programs Take Hold," HHS Press Release, March 16, 2000, http://www.hhs.gov/news/press/2000pres/20000316.html.

208 Boyles, "Most Chicken Harbors Harmful Bacteria."

209 *Modern Meat.*

210 *Ibid.*

211 "Dirty Birds." *Consumer Reports.*

212 P.M. Cusack, M. McMeniman, and I.J. Lean, "The medicine and epidemiology of bovine respiratory disease in feedlots," *Australian Veterinary Journal* 81 (August 2003): 480–487.

213 Committee on Drug Use in Food Animals, Panel on Animal Health, Food Safety, and Public Health, National Research Council, *The Use of Drugs in Food Animals: Benefits and Risks* (Washington, D.C.: National Academy Press, 1999), 115.

214 *Ibid.*, 117.

215 *Ibid.*, 69.

216 *Ibid.*, 72–75.

217 *Modern Meat.*

218 Quoted in "The Future of Animal Protein in Poultry Diets," paper presented at Multi-State Poultry Meeting, May 14–16, 2002.

219 Vicki Lee Parker, "It Began With Chicken Feathers," North Carolina State Technology Incubator, January 2007, http://techincubator.ncsu.edu/news/BioResourceInternational_jan07.htm.

220 Gary G. Pearl, D.V.M., "The Future of Animal Protein Poultry Diets," paper presented at Multi-State Poultry Meeting, May 14–16, 2002.

221 Quoted in Thomas, "How Now Mad Cow."

222 Nestle, *Safe Food*, 46.

223 Quoted in Craig Reed, "Green Grass Grows Valuable Beef," *Oregon News*, March 22, 2007, http://www.oregonnews.com/article/20070322/NEWS/70322027.

224 Ellin Doyle, Ph.D., "Human Safety of Hormone Implants for Cattle Growth: A Review of the Scientific Literature," Food Research Institute, University of Wisconsin, 2000.

225 *Ibid.*

226 *Ibid.*

227 Gary C. Smith, "Meat Safety," paper presented at the Minnesota Dietary Association State Conference, March 19, 1999, http://ansci.colostate.edu/files/meat_science/meatsafety.pdf.

228 FDA Center for Veterinary Medicine, "The Use of Steroid Hormones for Growth Promotion in Food-Producing Animals," July 2002, http://www.fda.gov/cvm/hormones.htm.

229 Quoted in Todd S. Purdom, "Meat Inspections Face Overhaul, First in Nearly a Century," *New York Times*, July 7, 1996.

230 *Modern Meat.*

231 *Ibid.*

232 *Ibid.*

233 U.S. Department of Health and Human Services, "Fewer Americans Suffer From Foodborne Illnesses as Food Safety Programs Take Hold."

234 Quoted in Eleanor Clift, "Washington Report: How Safe Is Our Meat?" *Longevity*, June 1994, 74.

Conclusion: More Debates

235 Gurney Williams III, "What's Wrong With Fish?" *Vegetarian Times*, August 1995, 54–59.

236 See: Janet M. Torpy, "Eating Fish: Health Benefits and Risks," *Journal of the American Medical Association*, October 16, 2006, http://jama.ama-assn.org/cgi/content/full/296/15/1926. See also: "Feds Recommend Fish-Eating Limits," CBS News Healthwatch, March 19, 2004, http://www.cbsnews.com/stories/2003/12/10/health/main587833.shtml; Harvard School of Public Health, "New Study Shows Benefits of Eating Fish Greatly Outweigh the Risks," October 17, 2006.

237 Paula Kurtzweil, "Critical Steps Toward Safer Seafood," *FDA Consumer*, November-December 1997, http://www.cfsan.fda.gov/~dms/fdsafe3.html.

238 Quoted in Williams III, "What's Wrong With Fish?" 56.

239 "Safety of Cow Growth Hormone Disputed," *The Healthy Cell News*, Spring/Summer 1995, 12.

240 *Ibid.*

241 Susan Gilbert, "Fears Over Milk, Long Dismissed, Still Simmer," *New York Times*, January 19, 1999.

242 S.E. Hankinson, et al., "Circulating concentrations of insulin-like growth factor 1 and risk of breast cancer," *Lancet* 351, no. 9113 (1998): 1393–1396. See also: June M. Chan, et al., "Plasma Insulin-Like Growth Factor-1 [IGF-1] and Prostate Cancer Risk: A Prospective Study," *Science*, January 23, 1998, 563–566.

243 Francesca Lyman, "MSNBC Reopens Debate on Safety of Bovine Growth Hormone in Milk," March 29, 2006, http://www.purefood.org/rbgh/msnbconrbgh.cfm.

244 *Ibid.*

245 Bruce Mohl, "2 Dairies to end use of artificial hormones," *Boston Globe*, September 26, 2006, http://www.boston.com/business/articles/2006/09/25/2_dairies_to_end_use_of_artificial_hormones.

246 Teitel and Wilson, *Genetically Engineered Food*, 37.

247 Malinda Geisler, "Organic Dairy Profile," Agricultural Marketing Resource Center, November 2006, http://www.agmrc.org/agmrc/commodity/livestock/dairy/organicdairyprofile.htm.

248 Goldstein, *Demanding Clean Food and Water*, 115.

249 *Ibid.*, 113.

250 For more about these debates, see: Null, *Clearer, Cleaner, Safer, Greener*, 66; "Fluoridation Debate," *Environmental Health Perspectives*, November 1997, 1176; Fluoride Action Network, http://www.FluorideAction.Net; and Fluoride Debate, http://www.fluoridedebate.com.

251 Food and Drug Administration, "USDA Issues Final Rule on Meat and Poultry Irradiation," December 1999, http://www.fsis.usda.gov/OA/background/irrad_final.htm.

252 Ibid.

253 Quoted in Russell Clemings, "Sizzling Up a Safer Burger," *Longevity*, June 1994, 66.

254 Jacobson, Lefferts, and Garland, *Safe Food*, 102.

255 Clemings, "Sizzling Up a Safer Burger."

256 "USDA Issues Final Rule on Meat and Poultry Irradiation," February 2000.

257 Russell L. Blaylock, M.D., *Excitotoxins: The Taste That Kills* (Albuquerque, N.M.: Health Press, 1996), 27, 29, 38–56.

258 J.W. Olney, "Brain lesions, obesity, and other disturbances in mice treated with monosodium glutamate." *Science*, 1969, 719–721.

259 "FDA Limits Red Dye No. 3," *New York Times*, January 30, 1990.

260 John Henkel, "From Shampoo to Cereals: Seeing to the Safety of Color Additives," *FDA Consumer*, December 1993.

261 Pallavi Gogoi, "An Insider's Guide to Food Labels," *Business Week*, October 6, 2006, http://www.businessweek.com/bwdaily/dnflash/content/aug2006/db20060807_789872.htm?chan=search.

262 Food and Drug Administration, "Genetically Engineered Foods: Fears and Facts," January/February 1993, http://www.fda.gov/bbs/topics/consumer/Con00191.html.

263 Noel C. Paul, "Where's the Beef (from)?" *Christian Science Monitor*, April 14, 2003, http://www.csmonitor.com/2003/0414/p17s01-wmcn.html.

264 For more information, see: Barry Krissoff, Fred Kuchler, Kenneth Nelson, Janet Perry, and Agapi Somwaru,

"Country-of-Origin Labeling: Theory and Observation," USDA Economic Research Service (ERS), report, January 2004, http://www.ers.usda.gov/publications/WRS04/jan04/wrs0402; Country of Origin Labeling (viewpoints from food industry coalition), http://www.countryoforiginlabel.org.

265 Scott Gottlieb, M.D., "How Safe Is Our Food? FDA Could Do Better," *USA Today*, May 21, 2007.

266 Quoted in Matthews, "NY Sen. Schumer says loose federal oversight puts food supply at risk."

267 *Ibid.*

268 "Durbin, DeLauro Introduce New Food Safety Bill in Wake of Widening Recalls," May 1, 2007, http://durbin.senate.gov/record.cfm?id=273386.

269 Nestle, *Safe Food*, 27–28.

RESOURCES

Books

Avery, Dennis. *Saving the Planet With Pesticides and Plastic: The Environmental Triumph of High-Yield Farming.* Washington, D.C.: Hudson Institute, 2000.

Avise, John C. *The Hope, Hype and Reality of Genetic Engineering: Remarkable Stories from Agriculture, Industry, Medicine and the Environment.* New York: Oxford University Press, 2004.

Bailey, Ronald. *Liberation Biology: The Scientific and Moral Case for the Biotech Revolution.* Amherst, N.Y.: Prometheus Books, 2005.

Berlau, John. *EcoFreaks: Environmentalism Is Hazardous to Your Health!* Nashville, Tenn.: Thomas Nelson, 2006.

Blaylock, Russell L., M.D. *Excitotoxins: The Taste That Kills.* Albuquerque, N.M.: Health Press, 1996.

Boyens, Ingeborg. *Unnatural Harvest: How Corporate Science Is Secretly Altering Our Food.* Garden City, N.Y.: Doubleday Books, 1999.

Carson, Rachel. *Silent Spring.* London: Readers Union, 1964.

Cook, Christopher. *Diet for a Dead Planet: Big Business and the Coming Food Crisis.* New York: The New Press, 2006.

Davis, Karen. *Prisoned Chickens, Poisoned Eggs: An Inside Look at the Modern Poultry Industry.* Summertown, Tenn.: Book Publishing, 1996.

Dean, J.H., and M. Padaranth Singh, eds. *Biological Relevance of Immune Suppression.* New York: Van Nostrand Reinhold, 1981.

Eisnitz, Gail A. *Slaughterhouse: The Shocking Story of Greed, Neglect, and Inhumane Treatment Inside the U.S. Meat Industry.* Amherst, N.Y.: Prometheus, 1997.

Fox, Nicols. *Spoiled: The Dangerous Truth About a Food Chain Gone Haywire.* New York: Penguin, 1998.

Goldstein, Joan. *Demanding Clean Food and Water.* New York: Plenum Publishing, 1990.

Hart, Kathleen. *Eating in the Dark: America's Experiment with Genetically Engineered Food.* New York: Pantheon Books, 2002.

Hawthorne, Fran. *Inside the FDA: The Business and Politics Behind the Drugs We Take and the Food We Eat.* Hoboken, N.J.: John Wiley & Sons, 2005.

Jacobson, Michael F., Lisa Y. Lefferts, and Anne Witte Garland. *Safe Food: Eating Wisely in a Risky World.* Los Angeles: Living Planet Press, 1991.

Kneen, Brewster. *Farmageddon: Food and the Culture of Biotechnology.* Gabriola Island, B.C., Canada: New Society Publishers, 1999.

Lappe, Francis Moore, Joseph Collins, and Peter Rosset. *World Hunger: Twelve Myths.* New York: Grove/Atlantic Press, 1998.

Lyman, Howard F. *No More Bull! The Mad Cowboy Targets America's Worst Enemy: Our Diet.* New York: Scribner's, 2005.

McKelway, Ben, ed. *Guess What's Coming to Dinner: Contaminants in Our Food.* Washington, D.C.: Center for Science in the Public Interest (CSPI), 1987.

Midkiff, Ken. *The Meat You Eat: How Corporate Farming Has Endangered America's Food Supply.* New York: St. Martin's Griffin Press, 2005.

Nestle, Marion. *Food Politics: How the Food Industry Influences Nutrition and Health.* Berkeley: University of California Press, 2003.

————. *Safe Food: Bacteria, Biotechnology, and Bioterrorism.* Berkeley: University of California Press, 2004.

Null, Gary. *Clearer, Cleaner, Safer, Greener: A Blueprint for Detoxifying Your Environment.* New York: Random House, 1990.

Pimentel, David, ed., *CRC Handbook of Pest Management in Agriculture.* 2nd ed. Vol. 1. London: CRC Press, 1990.

Pollan, Michael. *The Omnivore's Dilemma: A Natural History of Four Meals.* New York: Penguin, 2006.

Pringle, Peter. *Food, Inc.* New York: Simon & Schuster, 2003.

Rampton, Sheldon, and John Stauber. *Mad Cow U.S.A.: Could the Nightmare Happen Here?* Monroe, Maine: Common Courage Press, 1997.

Rissler, Jane, and Margaret Mellon. *The Ecological Risks of Engineered Crops.* Cambridge, Mass.: MIT Press, 1996.

Shiva, Vandana. *Stolen Harvest: The Hijacking of the Global Food Supply.* Cambridge, Mass.: South End Press, 1999.

Striffler, Steve. *Chicken: The Dangerous Transformation of America's Favorite Food.* New Haven, Conn.: Yale University Press, 2005.

Stull, Donald D., Michael J. Broadway, and David Griffith, eds. *Any Way You Cut It: Meat Processing and Small-Town America.* Lawrence: University Press of Kansas, 1995.

Teitel, Martin, and Kimberly A. Wilson. *Genetically Engineered Food: Changing the Nature of Nature.* Rochester, Vt.: Park Street Press, 2001.

Articles and Reports

Ames, Bruce N., Renae Magaw, and Lois Swirsky Gold. "Ranking Possible Carcinogenic Hazards." *Science,* April 17, 1987, 271–280.

Beasley, Conger, Jr. "Of Pollution and Poverty." *Buzzword: The Environmental Journal*, May-June 1990, 40, 42.

Behar, Richard, and Michael Kramer. "Something Smells Fowl." *Time*, October 17, 1994, 43.

Benbrook, Charles. "Evidence of the Magnitude and Consequences of the Roundup Ready Soybean Yield Drag from University-Based Varietal Trials in 1998." Ag BioTech InfoNet Technical Paper, No. 1, July 13, 1999. Available online. URL: http://www.biotech-info.net/herbicide-tolerance.html. Accessed June 27, 2007.

Boyles, Salynn. "Most Chicken Harbors Harmful Bacteria." WebMD Medical News, December 4, 2006. Available online. URL: http://www.medicinenet.com/script/main/art.asp?articlekey=77924. Accessed June 27, 2007.

Bren, Linda. "Genetic Engineering: The Future of Foods?" *FDA Consumer Magazine*, November/December 2003. Available online. URL: http://www.fda.gov/fdac/features/2003/603_food.html.

Brink, Susan, and Nancy Shute. "Is It Safe?" *U.S. News and World Report*, January 4, 2004. Available online. URL: http://www.usnews.com/usnews/news/articles/040112/12cow_2.htm. Accessed June 27, 2007.

Burros, Marian. "Experts Concerned About Return of Deadly Bacteria in Cold Cuts." *New York Times*, March 14, 1999.

———. "Is That Food Really Safe?" *New York Times*, March 15, 1989, C1, C4.

Clemings, Russell. "Sizzling Up a Safer Burger." *Longevity*, June 1994, 66.

Clift, Eleanor. "Washington Report: How Safe Is Our Meat?" *Longevity*, June 1994, 64, 66, 74.

Committee on Drug Use in Food Animals, Panel on Animal Health, Food Safety, and Public Health, National Research Council. *The Use of Drugs in Food Animals: Benefits and Risks*. Washington, D.C.: The National Academies Press, 1999.

Cowley, Geoffrey, and John McCormick. "How Safe Is Our Food?" *Newsweek*, May 24, 1993, 52–58.

Davis, K.L., J.A. Savage, and P.A. Berger. "Possible Organophosphate Induced Parkinsonism." *Journal of Mental Nervous Disorder* 66 (1978): 222–225.

DePalma, Anthony, and Bruce Lambert. "Gumshoe Work and Some Luck Helped Pinpoint Suspected Source of *E. Coli*." *New York Times*, December 10, 2006, 45, 48.

Doyle, Ellin, Ph.D. "Human Safety of Hormone Implants for Cattle Growth: A Review of the Scientific Literature." Food Research Institute, University of Wisconsin, 2000.

Eskin, Sandra B., Nancy Donley, Donna Rosenbaum, and Karen Taylor Mitchell. *Why Are People Still Dying From Contaminated Food?* Report from Safe Tables Our Priority (STOP), February 2003. Available online. URL: http://www.safetables.org/pdf/STOP_Report.pdf. Accessed June 27, 2007.

Fitzgerald, Beth. "Jersey Lab Splices Veggie Gene." *Sunday Star-Ledger*, July 4, 1993, Section 3, pp. 5, 6.

Foulke, Judith E. "FDA Reports on Pesticides in Foods." *FDA Consumer*, June 1993.

Geisler, Malinda. "Organic Dairy Profile." Agricultural Marketing Resource Center, November 2006. Available online. URL: http://www.agmrc.org/agmrc/commodity/livestock/dairy/organicdairyprofile.htm. Accessed June 27, 2007.

Gilbert, Susan. "America Tackles the Pesticide Crisis." *New York Times Magazine*, October 8, 1989, 51.

Gogoi, Pallavi. "An Insider's Guide to Food Labels." *Business Week*, October 6, 2006. Available online. URL: http://www.businessweek.com/bwdaily/dnflash/content/aug2006/db20060807_789872.htm?chan=search. Accessed June 27, 2007.

Gottlieb, Scott, M.D. "How Safe Is Our Food? FDA Could Do Better." *USA Today*, May 21, 2007.

Grossfeld, Stan. "Animal Waste Emerging as U.S. Problem." *Boston Globe*, September 21, 1998.

Hinsdill, R.D., D.L. Couch, and R.S. Speirs. "Immunosuppression Induced by Dioxin (TCDD) in Feed." *Journal of Environmental Toxicology* 4 (1980): 401.

Hoar, Sheila, et al. "Agricultural Herbicide Use and Risk of Lymphoma and Soft-Tissue Sarcoma." *Journal of the American Medical Association*, September 5, 1986, 1141–1147.

Hord, Bill. "Researcher Seeks New Ways to Feed Hungry World." *Omaha World-Herald*, April 11, 2007. Available online. URL: http://www.omaha.com/index.php?u_page=1208&u_sid=2363093. Accessed June 27, 2007.

Knickerbocker, Brad. "Third Mad Cow Case in US Raises Questions About Testing." *Christian Science Monitor*, March 15, 2006. Available online. URL: http://www.csmonitor.com/2006/0315/p02s01-uspo.html. Accessed June 27, 2007.

Krissoff, Barry, Fred Kuchler, Kenneth Nelson, Janet Perry, and Agapi Somwaru. "Country-of-Origin Labeling: Theory and Observation." USDA Economic Research Service (ERS) report, January 2004. Available online. URL: http://www.ers.usda.gov/publications/WRS04/jan04/wrs0402. Accessed June 27, 2007.

"Let Nature's Harvest Continue!" African Counter Statement to Monsanto, at the 5th Extraordinary Session of the FAQ Commission on Genetic Resources, June 12, 1998.

Maryanski, James. Statement Before the Senate Committee on Agriculture, Nutrition, and Forestry, October 7, 1999.

McCammon, Sally. "Regulating Products of Biotechnology." *Economic Perspectives* 4, no. 4 (October 1999).

Mothers and Others For Pesticide Limits. *Pesticides in Children's Food.* Washington, D.C.: National Resources Defense Council (NRDC), 1989.

O'Neill, Molly. "Organic Industry Faces An Ethics Question." *New York Times*, May 17, 1995, C1, C6.

Paulson, Amanda. "As Organic Goes Mainstream, Will Standards Suffer?" *Christian Science Monitor*, May 17, 2006. Available online. URL: http://www.csmonitor.com/2006/0517/p13s01-lifo.html. Accessed June 27, 2007.

Pearl, Gary G., D.V.M. "The Future of Animal Protein Poultry Diets." Paper presented to Multi-State Poultry Meeting, May 14–16, 2002.

Pollak, Andrew. "Altered Crops Draw Protests, Pro and Con." *New York Times*, December 14, 1999, A-25.

———. "Biotech's Sparse Harvest: A Gap Between the Lab and the Dining Table." *New York Times*, February 14, 2006, C-1.

———. "Monsanto Buying Leader in Fruit and Vegetable Seeds." *New York Times*, January 25, 2005, C-7.

Potrykus, Ingo. "Golden Rice and Beyond." *Plant Physiology*, March 2001, 1157–1161.

———. "Response to Golden Rice Critics." *AgBioWorld* 28 (June 2000).

Pretty, Jules. "Feeding the World?" *SPLICE* 4, no. 6 (August-September, 1998). Available online. URL: http://ngin.tripod.com/article2.htm. Accessed June 27, 2007.

Public Employees for Environmental Responsibility (PEER). "Genetic Genie: The Premature Commercial Release of Genetically Engineered Bacteria." Washington, D.C.: PEER, September 1995.

Ralli, Tania. "Modified Food Labeling Begins in Europe." *New York Times,* April 21, 2004, F-6.

Rinsky, R.A., et al. "Benzene and Leukemia." *New England Journal of Medicine* 316 (1987): 1044–1050.

Rosen, Joseph D. "Much Ado About Alar." *Issues in Science and Technology,* Fall 1990, 85–90.

Rosset, Peter. "Why Genetically Altered Food Won't Conquer Hunger." *New York Times,* September 1, 1999.

Sachs, Jessica Snyder. "Hidden Dangers in Your Food and Water." *McCalls,* August 1994, 40, 46.

Schardt, David, and Stephen Schmidt. "Keeping Food Safe," *Nutrition Health Newsletter,* April 1995, 4–7.

Schneider, Keith. "Farm Debate to Center on Pesticides." *New York Times,* January 10, 1990, A-25.

Shapin, Steven. "Paradise Sold." *New Yorker,* May 15, 2006. Available online. URL: http://www.newyorker.com/archive/2006/05/15/060515crat_atlarge. Accessed June 27, 2007.

Shapiro, Laura, et al. "Suddenly, It's a Panic for Organics." *Newsweek,* March 27, 1989, 24, 26.

Smith, R.J. "Hawaiian milk contamination creates alarm, a sour response by regulators." *Science,* 1982, 137–140.

Thomas, Cathy Booth. "How Now, Mad Cow?" *Time,* January 3, 2004. Available online. URL: http://www.time.com/time/magazine/article/0,9171,1101040112-570218,00.html. Accessed June 27, 2007.

Union of Concerned Scientists. "What's in the Meat You Eat?" October 2003. Available online. URL: http://www.ucsusa.org/publications/greentips/1003-whats-in-the-meat-you-eat.html. Accessed June 27, 2007.

U.S. Centers for Disease Control and Prevention. "Preliminary Food-Net Data on the Incidence of Foodborne Illnesses." April 19, 2002.

Available online. URL: http://www.cdc.gov/mmwr/preview/mmwrhtml/mm5115a3.htm. Accessed June 27, 2007.

U.S. Environmental Protection Agency. *List of Chemicals Evaluated for Carcinogenic Potential.* Washington, D.C.: EPA, 1990.

U.S. Food and Drug Administration. "Genetically Engineered Foods: Fears and Facts." January/February 1993. Available online. URL: http://www.fda.gov/bbs/topics/consumer/Con00191.html. Accessed June 27, 2007.

Youngberg, Garth. *Report and Recommendation on Organic Farming.* Washington, D.C.: U.S. Department of Agriculture (USDA), 1980.

Web sites
Centers for Disease Control and Prevention (CDC)
http://www.cdc.gov
Statistics and general information about food-borne illnesses and reports on specific outbreaks.

Council for Biotechnology Information
http://www.whybiotech.com
A site devoted to showing the benefits of genetic engineering of plants, including food crops.

Council For Responsible Genetics (CRG)
http://www.gene-watch.org
CRG aims to encourage "public debate about the social, ethical, and environmental implications of genetic technologies" and "to distribute accurate information and represent the public interest on emerging issues in biotechnology."

Environmental Protection Agency (EPA)
http://www.epa.gov
Official government Web site contains information about regulations and enforcement of laws affecting air, water, soil, and crops as they affect the environment and human health. Specific information about pesticides at www.epa.gov/pesticides.

The Golden Rice Project
http://www.goldenrice.org
Information about the bioengineered, nutritionally enhanced rice discussed in Chapters 4 and 5, including how the rice was developed and its use in poor countries.

Greenpeace
http://www.greenpeace.org/usa/campaigns/toxics
Nonprofit organization that works to ban the use of various agricultural and industrial chemicals considered by some to be hazardous to the environment and human health.

Soil and Water Conservation Society

http://www.swcs.org

Information and resources relating to "the natural art and science of natural resource management for sustainability."

U.S. Department of Agriculture (USDA)

http://www.usda.gov

USDA Animal and Plant Health Inspection Service (APHIS): Biotechnology

http://www.aphis.usda.gov/biotechnology/brs_main.shtml

Information about how the nation regulates genetically engineered plants and animals, including discussion on how the agency enforces regulations regarding genetically engineered organisms.

U.S. Food and Drug Administration (FDA)

http://www.fda.gov

U.S. FDA Center for Food Safety and Applied Nutrition (CFSAN)

http://www.cfsan.fda.gov

Information about the history, functions, and activities of the CFSAN; includes reports on foods and drugs and the science behind regulatory decisions.

World Health Organization (WHO)

http://www.who.org

Legislation

Federal Food and Drugs Act of 1906 ("Wiley Act"), Public Law 59-384

The nation's first major federal food safety law was passed to prevent "the manufacture, sale, or transportation of adulterated or misbranded or poisonous or deleterious foods, drugs, medicines, and liquors, and for regulating traffic therein . . ."

Federal Meat Inspection Act 1906

This federal law mandated that the Department of Agriculture inspect meat products in the form of livestock before slaughter and as carcasses, and to refuse to approve products that did not pass inspection.

Federal Food, Drug, and Cosmetic Act 1938

With this law, Congress expanded the scope of the 1906 act by extending federal authority to cosmetics and therapeutic devices and setting stricter standards for drugs.

In the area of food safety, the act authorized factory inspections and added the remedy of court injunctions to the previous penalties (seizures and prosecutions) that were used to gain compliance.

Miller Pesticide Amendment 1954

This amendment to the 1938 food and drug act specified the procedures for setting safety limits for pesticide residues on raw agricultural products. This responsibility was first assigned to the FDA but was transferred to the EPA in 1970.

Food Additives Amendment 1958

This amendment required manufacturers of new food additives to establish their safety. The section known as the Delaney clause prohibited the approval of any food additive that was shown to induce cancer in people or animals.

Color Additive Amendment 1960

Similar to the food additives amendment, this law required manufacturers to establish the safety of color additives used in foods, drugs, and cosmetics, with the Delaney clause banning the approval of any color additive that was shown to induce cancer in people or animals.

Nutrition, Labeling and Education Act 1990

Requires that all packaged foods contain labels listing ingredients and nutritional content consistent with terms set forth by the secretary of Health and Human Services. An amendment in 2003 required food producers to list trans fat content in foods.

Food, Agriculture, Conservation, and Trade Act of 1990 (FACTA), Public Law 101-624.

Provisions of this act require users of restricted-use pesticide products to keep records showing the name and amount of pesticide used, date used, specific location where it was applied, and other information.

Food Quality Protection Act 1996

This amendment to the 1938 act eliminated the Delaney clause as applied to pesticide residues on foods. It states that the EPA must be able to conclude with "reasonable certainty that no harm will result from aggregate exposure" to each pesticide from dietary and other sources. This law also takes into account the special vulnerabilities of infants and children to pesticide exposure.

Federal Insecticide, Fungicide, and Rodenticide Act (FIFRA) 1996

This act provides for federal control of pesticide distribution, sale, and use. The EPA, which registers all pesticides for use in the United States, has authority to study the results of pesticide usage and to require users to register when purchasing pesticides. Amendments to the law require users to take exams to be certified as applicators of pesticides.

Food Allergy Labeling and Consumer Protection Act 2004

Requires food producers to label any food that contains a protein derived from any of the following food groups, which are known to cause the vast majority of allergic reactions: peanuts, tree nuts, cow's milk, soybeans, eggs, fish, shellfish, and wheat.

Cases

U.S. v. Lexington Mill & Elevator Co., 232 U.S. 399 (1914)

In its first ruling on food additives, the Supreme Court said the government could not ban the use of bleached flour with nitrate residues in foods. In order to ban a chemical additive, the court said, the government must show a relationship between that additive and the harm it allegedly caused in humans. Furthermore, said the court, the mere presence of such an ingredient was not in itself sufficient to make a food illegal.

APHA v. Butz, 511 F. 2nd (1974)

The American Public Health Association (APHA) sued then-Secretary of Agriculture Earl Butz, claiming that the USDA stamp of approval was misleading because the USDA could not assure consumers that meat products were safe. APHA asked the department to require warning labels on meat and poultry alerting consumers to the presence of pathogens. The court ruled for the defendant, saying that such labels were unnecessary, and wrote, "American housewives and cooks normally are not ignorant or stupid and their methods of preparing and cooking of food do not ordinarily result in salmonellosis." The court also said that bacteria were inherent to meats and that USDA approval was not intended to promise that all products were pathogen-free.

Diamond v. Chakrabarty, 447 U.S. 303 (1980)

In 1980, the U.S. Supreme Court ruled that living cells can be patented under Title 35 U.S.C. 101, which provides for the issuance of a patent to a person who "invents or discovers any new and useful manufacture or composition of matter." This extended patent rights to include genetically engineered organisms (in this case a bacterium that was capable of breaking down crude oil, making it useful for dealing with oil spills.)

The court noted, "Respondent's micro-organism constitutes a 'manufacture' or 'composition of matter' within that statute." This decision has since been used to support the idea that people or corporations can own the rights to a living organism.

Les v. Reilly, **United States Court of Appeals, Ninth Circuit.** 968 F.2d 985 (1992)

Citing the Delaney clause, a group of citizens joined environmental groups and the AFL-CIO to sue the EPA for permitting the use of four pesticides that had been shown to cause cancer. The court ruled in their favor, saying:

> The language is clear and mandatory. The Delaney clause provides that no additive shall be deemed safe if it induces cancer. 21 U.S.C. 348(c)(3). The EPA states in its final order that appropriate tests have established that the pesticides at issue here induce cancer in humans or animals.

Geertson Seed Farms et al. v. Mike Johanns, **Civil Action C 06-01075, N.D. Cal., February 13, 2007**

A coalition of environmental organizations joined a grower in suing the Department of Agriculture's Animal and Plant Inspection Service (APHIS), saying that the agency failed to consider the full environmental impact before it approved the commercial use of Roundup Ready alfalfa, a genetically engineered crop from the Monsanto Company. Citing the possibility of genetic contamination of conventional and organic alfalfa crops, Judge Charles E. Breyer ruled in favor of the plaintiffs in what is expected to become an important decision in the debate over GM foods.

Terms and Concepts

"action levels"

adulteration

agribusiness

carcinogenic

coloring agent

conventional agriculture

country-of-origin labeling

"factory farm"

federal inspection

food-borne illness

food-borne pathogen

foreign gene

genetically modified (GM); also genetically engineered (GE)

growth hormone (synthetic)

Hazard Analysis and Critical Control Points (HACCP)

irradiation

line speeds

microbial testing

organic agriculture

pesticides, naturally occurring

pesticides, synthetic

reasonable certainty

recall

regulatory agency

resistant organism

safe handling instructions

sustainable agriculture

tolerance levels

transgenic organism

Beginning Legal Research

The goal of POINT/COUNTERPOINT is not only to provide the reader with an introduction to a controversial issue affecting society, but also to encourage the reader to explore the issue more fully. This appendix, then, is meant to serve as a guide to the reader in researching the current state of the law as well as exploring some of the public-policy arguments as to why existing laws should be changed or new laws are needed.

Like many types of research, legal research has become much faster and more accessible with the invention of the Internet. This appendix discusses some of the best starting points, but of course "surfing the Net" will uncover endless additional sources of information—some more reliable than others. Some important sources of law are not yet available on the Internet, but these can generally be found at the larger public and university libraries. Librarians usually are happy to point patrons in the right direction.

The most important source of law in the United States is the Constitution. Originally enacted in 1787, the Constitution outlines the structure of our federal government and sets limits on the types of laws that the federal government and state governments can pass. Through the centuries, a number of amendments have been added to or changed in the Constitution, most notably the first ten amendments, known collectively as the Bill of Rights, which guarantee important civil liberties. Each state also has its own constitution, many of which are similar to the U.S. Constitution. It is important to be familiar with the U.S. Constitution because so many of our laws are affected by its requirements. State constitutions often provide protections of individual rights that are even stronger than those set forth in the U.S. Constitution.

Within the guidelines of the U.S. Constitution, Congress—both the House of Representatives and the Senate—passes bills that are either vetoed or signed into law by the President. After the passage of the law, it becomes part of the United States Code, which is the official compilation of federal laws. The state legislatures use a similar process, in which bills become law when signed by the state's governor. Each state has its own official set of laws, some of which are published by the state and some of which are published by commercial publishers. The U.S. Code and the state codes are an important source of legal research; generally, legislators make efforts to make the language of the law as clear as possible.

However, reading the text of a federal or state law generally provides only part of the picture. In the American system of government, after the

legislature passes laws and the executive (U.S. President or state governor) signs them, it is up to the judicial branch of the government, the court system, to interpret the laws and decide whether they violate any provision of the Constitution. At the state level, each state's supreme court has the ultimate authority in determining what a law means and whether or not it violates the state constitution. However, the federal courts—headed by the U.S. Supreme Court—can review state laws and court decisions to determine whether they violate federal laws or the U.S. Constitution. For example, a state court may find that a particular criminal law is valid under the state's constitution, but a federal court may then review the state court's decision and determine that the law is invalid under the U.S. Constitution.

It is important, then, to read court decisions when doing legal research. The Constitution uses language that is intentionally very general—for example, prohibiting "unreasonable searches and seizures" by the police—and court cases often provide more guidance. For example, the U.S. Supreme Court's 2001 decision in *Kyllo* v. *United States* held that scanning the outside of a person's house using a heat sensor to determine whether the person is growing marijuana is unreasonable—*if* it is done without a search warrant secured from a judge. Supreme Court decisions provide the most definitive explanation of the law of the land, and it is therefore important to include these in research. Often, when the Supreme Court has not decided a case on a particular issue, a decision by a federal appeals court or a state supreme court can provide guidance; but just as laws and constitutions can vary from state to state, so can federal courts be split on a particular interpretation of federal law or the U.S. Constitution. For example, federal appeals courts in Louisiana and California may reach opposite conclusions in similar cases.

Lawyers and courts refer to statutes and court decisions through a formal system of citations. Use of these citations reveals which court made the decision (or which legislature passed the statute) and when and enables the reader to locate the statute or court case quickly in a law library. For example, the legendary Supreme Court case *Brown* v. *Board of Education* has the legal citation 347 U.S. 483 (1954). At a law library, this 1954 decision can be found on page 483 of volume 347 of the U.S. Reports, the official collection of the Supreme Court's decisions. Citations can also be helpful in locating court cases on the Internet.

Understanding the current state of the law leads only to a partial understanding of the issues covered by the POINT/COUNTERPOINT series. For a fuller understanding of the issues, it is necessary to look at public-policy arguments that the current state of the law is not adequately addressing the issue.

Many groups lobby for new legislation or changes to existing legislation; the National Rifle Association (NRA), for example, lobbies Congress and the state legislatures constantly to make existing gun control laws less restrictive and not to pass additional laws. The NRA and other groups dedicated to various causes might also intervene in pending court cases: a group such as Planned Parenthood might file a brief *amicus curiae* (as "a friend of the court")—called an "amicus brief"—in a lawsuit that could affect abortion rights. Interest groups also use the media to influence public opinion, issuing press releases and frequently appearing in interviews on news programs and talk shows. The books in POINT/COUNTERPOINT list some of the interest groups that are active in the issue at hand, but in each case there are countless other groups working at the local, state, and national levels. It is important to read everything with a critical eye, for sometimes interest groups present information in a way that can be read only to their advantage. The informed reader must always look for bias.

Finding sources of legal information on the Internet is relatively simple thanks to "portal" sites such as FindLaw (*www.findlaw.com*), which provides access to a variety of constitutions, statutes, court opinions, law review articles, news articles, and other resources—including all Supreme Court decisions issued since 1893. Other useful sources of information include the U.S. Government Printing Office (*www.gpo.gov*), which contains a complete copy of the U.S. Code, and the Library of Congress's THOMAS system (*thomas.loc.gov*), which offers access to bills pending before Congress as well as recently passed laws. Of course, the Internet changes every second of every day, so it is best to do some independent searching. Most cases, studies, and opinions that are cited or referred to in public debate can be found online—and *everything* can be found in one library or another.

The Internet can provide a basic understanding of most important legal issues, but not all sources can be found there. To find some documents it is necessary to visit the law library of a university or a public law library; some cities have public law libraries, and many library systems keep legal documents at the main branch. On the following page are some common citation forms.

COMMON CITATION FORMS

Source of Law	Sample Citation	Notes
U.S. Supreme Court	*Employment Division* v. *Smith*, 485 U.S. 660 (1988)	The U.S. Reports is the official record of Supreme Court decisions. There is also an unofficial Supreme Court ("S. Ct.") reporter.
U.S. Court of Appeals	*United States* v. *Lambert*, 695 F.2d 536 (11th Cir.1983)	Appellate cases appear in the Federal Reporter, designated by "F." The 11th Circuit has jurisdiction in Alabama, Florida, and Georgia.
U.S. District Court	*Carillon Importers, Ltd.* v. *Frank Pesce Group, Inc.*, 913 F.Supp. 1559 (S.D.Fla.1996)	Federal trial-level decisions are reported in the Federal Supplement ("F. Supp."). Some states have multiple federal districts; this case originated in the Southern District of Florida.
U.S. Code	Thomas Jefferson Commemoration Commission Act, 36 U.S.C., §149 (2002)	Sometimes the popular names of legislation—names with which the public may be familiar—are included with the U.S. Code citation.
State Supreme Court	*Sterling* v. *Cupp*, 290 Ore. 611, 614, 625 P.2d 123, 126 (1981)	The Oregon Supreme Court decision is reported in both the state's reporter and the Pacific regional reporter.
State Statute	Pennsylvania Abortion Control Act of 1982, 18 Pa. Cons. Stat. 3203-3220 (1990)	States use many different citation formats for their statutes.

page:
   12: AP Images/Richard Green
   30: AP Images/Chris Kaeser
   49: AP Images/Joey Gardner
   71: AP Images/Jake O'Connell,
      Merrill Sherman

cover: AP Images

97: AP Images/Chris Kaeser
118: AP Images/Dan Delorenzo

VICTORIA SHERROW is a freelance writer and member of the Society of Children's Book Writers. She is also the author of many books for middle- and high-school readers, including *Great Scientists*, *Political Leaders*, and, in the POINT/COUNTERPOINT series, *Women in the Military*.

ALAN MARZILLI, M.A., J.D., lives in Washington, D.C., and is a program associate with Advocates for Human Potential, Inc., a research and consulting firm based in Sudbury, Mass., and Albany, N.Y. He primarily works on developing training and educational materials for agencies of the federal government on topics such as housing, mental health policy, employment, and transportation. He has spoken on mental health issues in 30 states, the District of Columbia, and Puerto Rico; his work has included training mental health administrators, nonprofit management and staff, and people with mental illnesses and their families on a wide variety of topics, including effective advocacy, community-based mental health services, and housing. He has written several handbooks and training curricula that are used nationally and as far away as the territory of Guam. He managed statewide and national mental health advocacy programs and worked for several public interest lobbying organizations while studying law at Georgetown University. He has written more than a dozen books, including numerous titles in the POINT/COUNTERPOINT series.